Israel's Story

Part One

Dianne Bergant, C.S.A.

LITURGICAL PRESS
Collegeville, Minnesota

www.litpress.org

Cover design by Ann Blattner.

1	2	3	4	5	6	7	8

Library of Congress Cataloging-in-Publication Data

Bergant, Dianne.
    Israel's story / Dianne Bergant.
        p.   cm.
    ISBN-13: 978-0-8146-3046-4 (pt. 1 : alk. paper)
    ISBN-10: 0-8146-3046-4 (pt. 1 : alk. paper)
    1. Jews—History—To 70 A.D.   2. Judaism—History—To 70 A.D.
  3. Bible. O.T.—History of Biblical events.   4. Palestine—History—To 70 A.D.
  I. Title.

DS121.B485 2006
220.9'5—dc22

                                                                2006003684

Contents

Introduction

The ways in which we make our introductions are often culturally determined. In some circles we provide our name and place of employment; in others we say which school we attended or are attending now. People are often identified as someone's daughter or son; indigenous people often include the name of the tribe or clan to which they belong. Depending upon the circumstances, we might use a title such as Dr. or Mrs. or Captain; in others we use only our first names. Introductions tell aspects about ourselves that we want others to know. They do not tell everything; they merely open us up to an acquaintanceship. It takes much more contact and a great deal of time to really get to know a person.

An introduction to the Bible is quite similar. It provides as much information as the writer thinks is necessary for the readers to become acquainted with the characters found in the biblical accounts. It gives some historical information about these people, from whom and from where they came, and it recounts some of the events in which they themselves were engaged. At times these biblical people seem to be distant and unfamiliar; at other times we might feel that we know them intimately. An introduction to the Bible is just that—an introduction. If we want to get to know the Bible better, we will have to spend much more time with it than is possible with this first step. An introduction is a good way to begin, though.

Just as it is necessary to understand a person's language if we hope to get to know that person, so we will need some grasp of the language of the Bible or the way its message is expressed; we will have to know how to read the Bible if we are going to become acquainted with it. Although it is one book, the Bible is really a kind of anthology, a collection of many books and many different forms of writing. It contains both prose and poetry, and we know that these two types of writing are read quite differently. Much of the Bible is narrative, that is, written in some kind of story form.

However, there are various kinds of stories. There is historical writing, fiction, myth, and saga, to name only a few different forms or genres. In order to discover the meaning of a particular passage, we must first know what kind of story we are reading. If we do not know this, we might expect historical accuracy of a myth or exaggeration in a narrative account. On the other hand, poetry is rich in creative images and metaphors. It is more like a snapshot, while narrative often traces a thought or event through to its conclusion.

The Bible also contains lists which may not appear to be very interesting but which are very important. These include genealogies, law codes, and census lists. There are also prayers, such as the psalms; oracles, which contain the word of God; and proverbs, or wise sayings. Each unique literary form must be read in its own proper way.

It does not take long for one who reads the Bible carefully to detect what appear to be discrepancies. For example, there are two stories of the creation of the human couple (Gen 1:26-28; 2:7, 22), and they are not at all the same. There are two accounts of the number of animals that Noah took with him into the ark (Gen 6:19-20; 7:2-3). In some places the mountain from which God gave the commandments is called Sinai (Exod 19:11); in other places it is Horeb (Deut 4:15). Finally, there are two versions of the commandments themselves (Exod 20:2-17; Deut 5:6-21).

These differing accounts are evidence of both literary and theological diversity. In other words, the Bible contains more than one version of many of the major traditions of ancient Israel, and whoever put these traditions together in the final form that has come down to us chose to include both versions rather than eliminate one version in favor of the other. The original versions of these traditions themselves grew out of the religious reflection of various groups of people who had distinct perspectives and who were making specific theological points at different times in Israel's history.

Scholars recognize four major points of view in the first part of the Bible, known to Christians as the Pentateuch (Greek for "five books"— Genesis, Exodus, Leviticus, Numbers, Deuteronomy) and to the Jewish community as Torah (Hebrew for "Law"). These traditions have come to be known as Yahwist (J from Jahwist, the German spelling); Elohist (E); Deuteronomist (D); and Priestly (P). In the past some interpreters delineated these traditions quite explicitly, going so far as to identify which verse belonged to which tradition. Within the recent past this overly specific approach has been discontinued. Nevertheless, because it is clear that the first five books of the Bible contain traditions that are obviously very different, the designations are still used, and the general distinctions that they provide continue to have value.

The Yahwist tradition (J) consists of an interpretation of some commonly held stories such as the story of the garden in Eden and the first sin, and stories of the earliest ancestors, Abraham and Sarah, Isaac and Rebekah, Jacob and his wives and sons. This version developed among the southern tribes of Israel, and it reflects their political and religious concerns. Its name is derived from its frequent use of the word "Yahweh," the personal name of the God of Israel. Scholars maintain that the Yahwist tradition took shape sometime around the tenth century B.C.

While the Elohist tradition (E) contains some stories not found elsewhere, such as Abraham's willingness to sacrifice his son Isaac, it also includes a second version of some of the other ancestral stories. It reflects the later perspective held by the northern tribes, and its name comes from *elohim,* the generic word for "god," which seems to be preferred in this tradition. This version is generally dated in the ninth century B.C. This first part of Israel's story is found in chapters 1 and 2 of the present volume.

The Deuteronomist (D) tradition interprets the historical tradition of Israel from its entrance into the land of promise through its exile in Babylon. It is so named because the covenant theology found in the Book of Deuteronomy is the lens through which this history is interpreted. Though the basic form of this story originated before the deportation of the Jews to Babylon in 587 B.C., its final form is dated after that catastrophic experience, in the early part of the sixth century B.C.

Finally, the Priestly tradition (P) is concerned with cultic matters. Though undoubtedly many of the cultic practices originated before the Babylonian exile, the final form appeared during the latter part of the sixth century B.C. While the traditions of J, E, and P are found within the Pentateuch, most scholars agree that the P tradition acts as a kind of framework within which the entire Pentateuch has been set. With the exception of the Book of Deuteronomy itself, very little, if any, D is included in the Pentateuch.

The D tradition is found in the Book of Joshua through the two Books of Kings. The stories found there also underwent a long process of development and reinterpretation. Sagas or hero stories grew up around certain extraordinary individuals or were associated with important events or places. At a much later time in history they were gathered and retold in such a way as to demonstrate how fidelity to God was blessed, while unfaithfulness was punished. This "national history" was probably edited and re-edited until it achieved the form that has come down to us today. This part of Israel's story is found in chapters 3 through 5 of this volume.

The development of the tradition, as described above, explains how the stories of the ancient Israelites were handed down generation after generation, shaped and reshaped so that they might address the needs of people through the ages. The form that has come down to us contains the theological perspective of the final editor (J, E, D, or P). In other words, a story about Abraham might actually reflect a concern of the people at the time of David. Or the account of the destruction of the city of Jericho may really contain a profound theological lesson for people living at a much later time.

It is important to have an acquaintance with the people found within the pages of the Bible and with the events of their lives to have a basic grasp of the way the message of the Bible is expressed. Such historical and literary understanding serves a still more important purpose, and that is to grasp the religious meaning of the biblical message. Historical and literary knowledge is meant to throw light on the theological meaning. Several important religious themes will surface again and again. They will help us to uncover glimpses of ancient Israel's characterization of God as well as its concept of its relationship with that God. We will discover how these people perceived God as present and active in their history, and we will uncover some of their ritual responses to God's care of them. We will see that their hopes and dreams, their successes and failures are all interpreted through the lens of their religion. We study the Bible, not to imitate these people, but to learn about God from them.

First Things First

In the beginning

The Bible opens with the phrase "In the beginning . . ." (Gen 1:1). In the beginning of what? In the beginning of time? This reference can hardly be to chronological time, for the events that are recorded in the stories immediately following could not have occurred in time as we know it. Light itself is created before there is a heavenly body that radiates it (1:3, 14). The human couple are created twice (1:27; 2:7, 28). In the second account the man is molded of clay and then life is blown into him; the woman is built from one of the man's bones. There is a tree that bears knowledge rather than fruit (2:17), and there is a serpent that talks (3:1). The sons of heaven mate with human women (6:2), and people live to be 969 years old (5:27). The world in which such marvels occur is not the world of space and time in which we live. The Hebrew construction from which "In the beginning" is translated is quite obscure. The biblical writer may have intended this so that those hearing or reading these stories would realize that there is more here than mere history.

There are certainly many historical references and points of geography in the first eleven chapters of the Book of Genesis, but the major form of story found there is myth, not history. Myth is not fairy tale. It is a very special kind of creative narrative that contains fundamental truth, truth that is not limited to one particular time or place or event or individual, as history might be. Myth deals with universal truth, truth that pertains to all people, though in very different ways, truth that flows from the essentials of life and death.

1

When we look at the stories in the first eleven chapters of the Book of Genesis, we realize that they describe struggles that all people face, regardless of gender, race, culture, or ethnic origin. They are the stories of "Everyman" and "Everywoman." Perhaps a way of understanding them might be an opening phrase such as "From the beginning . . ." rather than "In the beginning . . ." We might then say that, from the beginning, women and men have acted in ways that lead to disaster, and they have blamed each other for it; from the beginning, siblings have fought with and even killed each other; from the beginning, human beings have tried to act as if they had the power and wisdom of the gods. Rather than merely recount events in the history of ancient Israel, these stories uncover inclinations that move deep within every one of us. Perhaps these first chapters tell us that "In the beginning . . ." this is the way the human race turned out, and it has continued in this fashion even down to our own day.

What's in a name?

In traditional societies such as ancient Israel, names are very important. They contain some of the very essence of the person. They might identify the person's origin ("Adam" means "from the ground" [Gen 2:7]); the person's role in society ("Eve" means "mother of all the living" [3:20]; "Abraham" means "father of a host of nations" [17:5]); or the person's relationship with God ("Israel" means "one who struggled with God and survived" [32:29]). The significance of names of human beings will be seen when they are examined in the context of the stories of those individuals. In the beginning of this study, we will look closely at the names given to God.

There is no question about which names Israel used to refer to its God. Many of them are found throughout the pages of the Bible. What is not clear is at what time in Israel's history certain names were popular and others were not. Two of these designations appear in the first eleven chapters of Genesis. They are "God" and "Lord." The Hebrew word for "God" is really *Elohim*, the plural form of the word "god." The use of this word suggests that far back in its history Israel worshiped more than one god. It was only after a long process of theological assimilation of various and conflicting ideas about God that Israel developed its monotheistic faith. It retained some of the traditional language and imagery, even though the people understood that language and imagery differently. This is not unlike the phrase "God of gods" which we today sometimes use in official prayer, despite the fact that we do not believe that there is more than one

God. On occasion the Bible uses the title *El*, the singular form of the word *Elohim*. We are probably unaware of the difference in the original Hebrew because both words are translated in our Bibles as "God." Strictly speaking, this word is not a name but a designation or title.

The personal name of the God of Israel is Yahweh. In order to show respect for this name, most contemporary Bibles do not use it. Instead, they substitute the word "LORD" whenever the personal name appears in the text. This is not really a translation but a substitution made for the sake of reverence for the divine name. The printed form of this word should be noted. The entire word is in uppercase or capital letters. A second Hebrew word, *adonai*, is also translated "Lord." This is a very common word, which is sometimes, but not always, used to refer to God. It is not a divine name, and it is printed differently in most Bibles. This is not an insignificant point. Printing the name in this way carries on a long tradition that originated within the Jewish community, where even today the personal name of God is not pronounced.

Just what does God's personal name mean? We really are not sure. It appears to be a form of the verb "to be." We find this in the story of Moses. When he asks for God's name, the answer he receives is "I am who am . . . tell the Israelites: I AM sent me to you" (Exod 3:14). In this passage we find the verb but not the name itself. Some translate the name as "I am who I will be" or "I am who will be." Others believe that the ambiguity is a way of saying "My name is too sacred for you to know and to use indiscriminately." The Israelites believed that if they knew God's name, they might think that they had power over God. Therefore, the exact name is not revealed to them. What we do know from this passage is that here God's personal name is somehow associated with the deliverance of the people.

There is an additional point of confusion regarding the personal name of God. The passage from the Book of Exodus suggests that the name was unknown until the time of Moses. It is found, though, in the second account of creation (Gen 2:4b), long before Moses ever appears on the scene. As we move through the Bible, we will find many such instances of apparent contradiction. This is evidence of literary diversity discussed in the Introduction (see p. vi). In other words, the Bible contains more than one version of many of the major traditions of ancient Israel, and whoever put these traditions together in the final form chose not to resolve what appears to us to be a discrepancy.

Usually the name given to God says something about how the people understood God's presence and action in their lives. The generic word

"God" is a good choice for the first account of creation (Gen 1:1–2:4a). It suggests divine power and majesty, and the account describes just that. It is there that we see a God whose word alone is powerful enough to bring all things into being. This God is both an architect who builds a magnificent universe and an artist who decorates it. This is a God who has power over life and who brings it forth in a myriad of marvelous expressions. This is a God who fashions a human couple in the divine image, which means that they stand in the place of God, with responsibility for the rest of creation. It is up to them to live in harmony with the natural world, to safeguard its treasures, and to nurture the life within it.

In the second creation account and the story of the first sin (Gen 2:4b–3:24), God is depicted in a very different way. The focus there is on human beings and their world, not on the broader universe. In this narrative God interacts with them on a very personal level. In such an account, the use of the personal name of God (LORD) seems to be quite appropriate. God is intimately involved in the creation of the man and the woman, shaping him as a potter works the clay and fashioning her as a sculptor shapes a figure. God even speaks with them, issuing instructions and reprimanding them when they disregard them. This notion of a God who is close to human beings is a good counterbalance to the earlier picture of a God who operates from a distance. Neither perspective is adequate in itself, but together they provide a better understanding of this mysterious God.

The two accounts of the creation of the first couple are quite different, reflecting two distinct points of view. In the first account the man and the woman are created at the same time, and they are made in the image and after the likeness of God (1:27). The only distinction between them is gender; there is no hierarchy or domination/subordination, no differentiation of roles. Both are told to "be fertile and multiply; fill the earth and subdue it. Have dominion . . ." (1:28). "Subdue and have dominion" is royal language, pointing to the responsibility of the monarchy. Thus this first couple is made to function in the world as king and queen, but they are to function as images of God, not as autonomous gods.

In the ancient Near Eastern world, people set up concrete images of their gods. These were not idols, though eventually their symbolic character was lost and people began to look at them as actual gods. Originally they were only symbols that represented the sovereignty of the god. In other words, the image was set up where this sovereignty functioned. To say that the first man and woman are images of God was to insist that they represent where God is sovereign, not where they are sovereign. They are not to rule in a spirit of independence and autonomy. Though they are meant to exercise dominion over the rest of creation, they are to do it as God would do it, ensuring that the earth will be safeguarded and life upon it will be abundantly fruitful. Furthermore, as images of God, they are accountable to God for their behavior, for their stewardship.

Details in the second account tell us that this story has an agricultural context. The man is placed in a garden to till it (the verb comes from the Hebrew word that means "to serve") and to guard it. Most of the action of the story takes place in the garden. There is a play on words between *adam*, which means "earth creature," and *adamah*, the "ground" out of which the man is made (2:7). There is an intimate relationship between this "earth creature" and other creatures. Both the trees and the animals are made of the same ground (2:9, 19). The creation of the woman is no less imaginative. She is built up from a rib of the man. There is a play on words in the account of her creation as well: *ishah* ("woman") comes from *ish* ("man"). Built from his rib, she is no more inferior to him than he is inferior to the ground from which he is formed.

The literary artistry of this story and the continuation of the same imagery are seen in the verses that recount the punishment that the couple must endure because they both violated God's directive. The "earth creature" will suffer in his relationship with the ground, the substance of his origin; the woman will suffer in her relationship with the man, the substance of her origin. The same Hebrew word translated as "birth pangs" in one instance (2:16) and as "toil" in the other (2:17) is used to describe the respective suffering they will endure as they try to bring forth life. This is a remarkably creative myth, not a historical account. As a myth, it speaks to all people of all times.

The literature of other ancient civilizations provides ample evidence that Israel often appropriated some of the popular mythological stories that were current at the time and then interpreted them through its own religious lens. All cultures have creation stories, and accounts of a massive flood are numerous. What is important is the religious message that the story communicates, not the historical accuracy of the details. This second creation story describes the agriculturalist's close connection with the ground, human refusal to follow God's directives, and broken relationships. Unlike the gods of many of the other nations, Israel's God is not capricious, inflicting hardship on a whim. There is a reason for human suffering. All of these religious matters are described within these artistic stories.

The transgression in the garden is not the only time that God is forced to punish sinful individuals. Story after story recounts the unwillingness of women and men to follow God's directives. The account of Cain and Abel exemplifies the extent to which jealousy and revenge can drive a person (4:1-16). It is difficult to understand why God accepts Abel's offering but not Cain's. Perhaps this simply reflects the storyteller's preference for herders over agriculturists. The point of the story is Cain's reaction to Abel's good fortune, not their respective occupations. It should be noted that while God does punish Cain for his crime, God also protects him from the possible revenge of others. The "mark of Cain," whatever that might have meant, was not a punishment, as some have thought.

The power of God is also evident in the account of the flood (chs. 6–9). There we see God the creator exercising control over creation once again. Now, however, the waters of the world are used as a force of punishment for sin. Here too the distant creator is the intimate judge of human behavior. Still, God's regret for having created humankind is not absolute: "Noah found favor with the LORD" (6:8). A careful look at this story suggests that it might be considered a kind of second creation. As with the first creation account, God brings the world and the life within it out of chaos. The blessing given here (9:1, 7) is the same as the one found earlier in the first creation account (1:28). This story shows that despite its sinfulness, the human race is given a fresh new start. Furthermore, this second chance is formalized by means of a covenant, or solemn pact. This covenant may be made through Noah, but it is not made with him alone. It is made with the entire human race down through the ages ("with you and your descendants after you") and with all living creatures ("with every living creature that was with you"). (9:9-10).

If the waters of the flood symbolize the return of chaos, the bow in the sky represents victory over those forces. The story itself recounts a flood, and so within that story the bow in the sky suggests a rainbow. On another level, the story is much more than an account of a natural disaster; it signifies the battle between cosmic forces of evil and corresponding cosmic forces of good. In the ancient Near Eastern world, a warrior god, after vanquishing his enemy, had no more need of weapons of war, and so he hung up his bow and quiver of arrows. In an interesting way, this resembles the ending of early western adventure stories in which the hero defeats the villain or villains and then hangs up his guns to show that the battle is over and order is established. The bow is a sign of this covenant.

While cosmic chaos may be defeated, it is not totally destroyed. The forces of sin and evil continue to wreak havoc on earth. Intent on making names for themselves, people decide to build a tower that is meant to reach the heavens and give them direct access to God at any time and in any way they choose (11:1-9). This attempt to gain power and autonomy shows that they are no different than their ancestors Adam and Eve, who sought wisdom in a way forbidden by God. As happened in the beginning, here too God steps in and thwarts the audacious human plan. Or is it God's plan that is thwarted by this act of arrogance? God created a fabulous world, replete with riches and beauty, and God fashioned human beings to live in this world in relationship with God and with one another. Time and again these human beings fall short of the potential with which they were created; and time and again God takes steps to set things right. It seems that this is to no avail. One might be tempted to presume that God will give up and either start all over again or simply not bother with human creation. But that is not what happens. It seems that God has another plan, and it begins with a man called Abram.

The stories in the first chapters of Genesis have been primarily mythological in character, reminding us of selfish inclinations that exist in all of us. The stories of the major ancestors and their families that follow these chapters contain historical and geographical information. Somehow a connection must be made between these two blocks of very different kinds of material. The connection is accomplished by means of genealogies (11:10-32). A genealogy is a listing of names in chronological order that traces lineage. Genealogies are very important at certain times in life. People need to know their ancestry in order to claim inheritance. Nations that have been broken by war or natural disaster often use genealogies to reorganize their people. In some cultures genealogies establish and solidify one's place in the community. Here the genealogies connect Abram with some of the heroes described in the earlier chapters of Genesis. This both gives him legitimacy and suggests that from the very beginning God had plans for the human race, and these plans would be brought to fulfillment in one particular family, the family of Abram.

My father was a wandering Aramean (Genesis 12–50)

The people of Israel trace their roots back to a man who migrated from a Mesopotamian city named Haran. He is called from that city by a God who promises to make him a great nation and a source of blessings for others (12:2-3). Without much certainty as to the reliability of this deity and the promises made, Abram packs up his family and his possessions and sets out for a foreign land. The details in these ancestral stories may not be historically verifiable, but most scholars believe that the events recorded here reflect life as it was lived in the Fertile Crescent (a crescent-shaped region that extends from the eastern shore of the Mediterranean Sea to the Persian Gulf) sometime during the first half of the second millennium B.C.

The promise that Abram will be a great nation is repeated once he arrives in the land designated by the God who called him. Abram is told that he will have as many descendants as there are stars in the night sky (15:5). To this promise is added a promise of land. These promises are then sealed with a covenant, or solemn pact (15:18). This covenant is initiated by God and requires nothing of Abram. It is an unconditional covenant.

Abram is childless, though, so how is this promise to be fulfilled? In order to remedy Abram's childlessness, his wife Sarai suggests that he take her maidservant Hagar as his wife. Hagar conceives and bears a son, who is named Ishmael, which means "God has heard" (16:11). This boy is not considered a legitimate heir, though, for he is the son of an Egyptian slave. A suitable heir must be the son of Abram's lawful wife, not the offspring of a house-servant.

Sarai's barrenness is the result of age. She is past her childbearing years (18:12). This physical obstacle is probably a literary ploy by the storyteller used to keep the suspense of the story high: will Abram ever have a legitimate son? Will the promises of God finally be fulfilled? Sarai's barrenness also has religious significance. If Sarai does give birth—and we know that eventually she does—it will be a manifestation of divine power and not merely an example of the natural process of conception. Furthermore, should this happen, there will be no doubt in anyone's mind about the uniqueness of the child born. A son born of Sarai will show that God's plan cannot be impeded by any kind of human limitation.

A second and quite different version of the covenant pact made between God and Abram follows (17:1-14). Though the promise of land is included in the story, the primary focus in this version is on the promise of descendants. First, Abram's name is changed to Abraham, which means "father of a host of nations." This new name reinforces the promise of many descendants.

Secondly, God directs Abraham to perform a ritual that will remind the people of the covenant promise of descendants. The foreskin of every man is to be circumcised. This mark on the flesh is a sign of this covenant. Since circumcision is a ceremony practiced much later in Israel's history, mention of it here suggests that this detail has been included in the story by the storyteller, who lived long after the time of the ancestors. It is added in order to underscore the long-standing significance of circumcision. Just as the covenant made through Noah was between God and all life on earth, this covenant is not made with Abraham alone, but rather with him and through him with all of his descendants down through the ages. Despite the importance of this covenant, Abraham still does not have a fully legitimate heir.

Abraham's special relationship with God is seen in a story about hospitality. It is the account of the fate of Sodom and Gomorrah, two cities that down through the ages have been linked with lewd and lascivious conduct. Again and again Abraham intercedes on behalf of the people of these corrupt cities, appearing to bargain with God. Again and again God acquiesces to Abraham's pleas and relents from punishing them (18:16-33), but it is to no avail. Had there been ten righteous people in the two cities, they would have been spared. But not even ten could be found.

The account of the destruction of the cities is quite graphic. The basis of the story is the violation of the custom of hospitality, a practice that was necessary for survival in ancient nomadic societies. Lot welcomes heavenly travelers into his home and fulfills his duties as host, but the townspeople transgress the protocol that should have ensured the safety of the guests and make outrageous sexual demands. Lot's offer of his daughters in place of his guests may offend our modern sensibilities, but his decision lays bare both the gravity of the responsibilities of hospitality and the lowly status of daughters in this ancient society.

A very interesting story describes Abraham's extending hospitality to strangers who have come to him from out of the desert. His behavior toward them demonstrates some of the hospitality protocol expected of members of this ancient society. In conversation with Abraham, the visitors announce that Abraham's wife, whose name has been changed from Sarai to Sarah, will give birth within the year. When earlier God had promised Abraham a son through Sarah, Abraham laughed (17:17). When Sarah hears the men make this claim, she too laughs (18:17).

But the laugh is on them, for Sarah does indeed conceive and bear a son, who is named Isaac, which means "laughter" (21:5-6). This is the favored son. He is more than his mother's darling or his father's pet—he is the child upon who depends the fulfillment of God's promises. Everything will now have to be done to assure his privilege and to ensure his safety. It may sound very harsh to us, but if Ishmael poses a threat, he will have to be banished. And so he is sent away. God, however, saves him and promises to make him a great nation as well (21:13).

It is important to understand the social and religious significance of Isaac if we are to appreciate the horror that Abraham faces when told that this is the son God wants him to sacrifice. Many people are repulsed by Abraham's compliance with the directive to sacrifice his son. They cannot understand how a father could be willing to do so, and the notion that God would give such a command is even more disturbing. The biblical text says that "God put Abraham to the test" (22:1). We know that this is a test, but there is no indication in the story that Abraham does.

The point of the story has little to do with the image of God that surfaces here, an image of God as capricious and playing with parental devotion. This story is really about priorities. Abraham is told to choose between the son who will fulfill the promises made by God and the God who made the promises in the first place. We must remember, this is a child who was born of a man and a woman who were too old to be parents (17:17). If God can bring life out of bodies that no longer possess the power to give life, surely God can bring lifeless bodies back to life. There is no indication that Abraham thinks in this way. All he knows is that the God who made promises, and up to this point has kept the promises that were made, is asking something of him. What choice will Abraham make?

As the story comes to an end, our fears are abated. Abraham does as he is directed; his devotion to God is demonstrated. In the nick of time Isaac is spared, and the promise of numerous descendants is repeated (22:17-18). Only the behavior of God continues to be troubling. The question of why a loving and compassionate God can allow "bad things to happen to good people" remains unanswered. This question will be posed again in the Book of Job. The issue of innocent suffering has tormented believers down through the centuries, even to our own day. This story maintains that Abraham's dilemma is a test from God. Such an explanation may not satisfy us, but at this point in the biblical story, it is the only explanation we have.

The Bible contains very few stories about Isaac, other than the accounts of his extraordinary birth and his rescue from death at the hand of his father. One aspect of this tradition that is very important deals with Isaac's wife. Although Abraham and his family enjoy great prosperity in the land of Canaan and seem to have interacted amicably with the inhabitants of that land, Abraham does not want his son to take a wife from these people. Instead, he sends a servant to return to the land from which Abraham came and to arrange a marriage for Isaac with a woman from Abraham's own kindred. There will be no intermarriage for Isaac; the promise must be handed down within the family.

A second important feature of the story of Isaac's marriage is his wife Rebekah's sterility. Like Sarah before her, she is a woman who cannot give birth. Once again, this apparent obstacle has both literary and religious significance. It heightens the suspense of the story and sets the stage for a miraculous conception. The resolution of this dilemma is the same as before: human limitation cannot thwart the plan of God. Just as Isaac was the child through whom God's promises would be fulfilled, so his son will carry those promises into the future. However, Rebekah gives birth to twins. Which one will be the child of promise?

The account of the birth of Esau and Jacob clearly states that this is more than a story of the birth of two boys. Rebekah is told that "two nations are in your womb, two peoples are quarreling while still within you" (25:23). Who are these nations? The text itself tells us (25:24-26). The first born, Esau, is "reddish" (the Hebrew word *admoni* sounds very much like Edom, a nation located southeast of Israel). The child is also "hairy" (the Hebrew word is *sear*, an allusion to Seir, another name for Edom).

Jacob is the second born. Later in the biblical narrative his name will be changed to "Israel" (32:29). So, the boys Esau and Jacob represent the nations Edom and Israel respectively. The question is not yet answered: Which one will be the child of promise? In most cultures this honor goes to the firstborn. This was certainly the custom in ancient Israel. By rights, Esau is the heir of the promises. The story of Isaac's bestowal of the blessing unfolds in a surprising way.

Esau does not seem to take his birthright seriously, so Jacob is able to bargain it away from him (25:29-34). Jacob's craftiness becomes manifest in the way he is able to trick his father into giving him the blessing intended for Esau. Actually, the craftiness originates with Rebekah. While Isaac favors Esau, the firstborn, Rebekah prefers Jacob (25:28). The story does not give any clues as to why this is the case, but it does point out the importance of the woman in determining the way the promises will be fulfilled. She devises a plan to fool her husband Isaac and to snatch the blessing for the son who has already procured his brother's birthright (27:6ff.). The deception is carried off, and Jacob emerges successful. When it becomes clear what has happened, Esau is enraged and threatens to kill his brother upon the death of their father Isaac. But before Isaac dies, he instructs Jacob to return to the land of their ancestors and there to marry a woman of their own kindred rather than a Canaanite woman (28:1). Jacob follows his father's instructions and leaves. The conflict between the brothers is left unresolved.

The tradition surrounding Jacob includes many intriguing and religiously significant stories. One recounts the difficulty he endures in trying to win the wife he desires (29:15-30). He falls in love with Rachel, the daughter of Laban, the maternal uncle with whom he is living. Laban promises the hand of his daughter if Jacob will work for him for seven years. At the end of this period, Jacob marries Laban's daughter, only to discover that he has been given Leah, Laban's elder daughter. Jacob, the one who twice tricked his twin brother, has himself been tricked by his uncle. So Jacob agrees to work for seven more years in order to win the hand of Rachel. After fourteen years Jacob finally has the woman he has loved from the start. He also has Leah, his first wife, who proves to be quite fertile. She bears him six sons and a daughter, and her maidservant bears two sons in her name. In the meantime, Rachel is barren.

Once again we encounter the theme of the patriarch's barren wife. Though the wives of the patriarchs are sometimes referred to as matriarchs, there was never a true matriarchy in Israel. It was always a patriarchal society (*patēr*, meaning "father," and *archēs*, meaning "headed"), not a matriarchal one (*matēr*, meaning "mother," and *archēs*, meaning "headed"). This does not mean that the wives played a negligible role, though. Sarah safeguards the privilege of her son, and Rebekah secures the blessing for hers. In this story we have Rachel, a barren woman who, like Sarah before her, gives her husband her own maidservant for a wife. Two sons are born of this union. Eventually, "God remembered Rachel . . . heard her prayer . . . and made her fruitful" (30:22). The son born of her is named Joseph. Of all his children, Jacob favors Joseph, because he is the son of the woman he truly loves. Some years later Rachel dies giving birth to a second son, whom Jacob names Benjamin (35:18).

Although Jacob now has many children and has amassed a substantial fortune, he is not in the land promised to his father Isaac and before him to Isaac's father Abraham. Still, returning to that land will mean an encounter with the brother he cheated so long ago, the brother who threatened to kill him. Despite this, Jacob sets out on the long and dangerous trek back home. In order to reach the land of promise, he must cross through Seir, the country of Edom, the home of his brother Esau.

The night before this encounter takes place, Jacob has an unus experience. Having safely secured his wives and children and posses- sions across the Jabbok River, Jacob is accosted by a being, the identity of which is unclear. The text initially says that it was a man (32:25), but further on in the story this being is in some way associated with God (32:29). Furthermore, Jacob himself claims to have seen God face to face (32:31). It is at this time that his name is changed from Jacob to Israel, which means "I have struggled with God and survived." This encounter leaves its mark on Jacob/Israel. He is struck on the hip and develops a limp as a result. His body may have been weakened, but he has gained a new kind of strength.

The story of the reunion of the brothers is quite touching (33:1-17). Jacob approaches Esau with fear and trepidation, while Esau runs to his brother with joyful abandon. Jacob, the chosen one of God, speaks with humility and deference, while Esau is overflowing with sentiments of love. Jacob may have repented of his violation of Esau's rights, but it is Esau, the one who in the past was offended, who initiates the reconcilia- tion. He does this by acting out his forgiveness of his brother. The broth- ers are reunited; the nations are no longer warring. The promises are no longer in danger, and so the plan of God can move to the next step.

Israel in Egypt

Sibling rivalry is not a new phenomenon. Its destructive power is seen in the story of Cain and Abel and in that of Jacob and Esau. It is operative again among the sons of Jacob (37:1-36). Jacob's favoritism toward Joseph undermines the relationship between that son and his older brothers. The stunning, colorful coat that Jacob gives his son ex- emplifies this paternal partiality.

Joseph's own behavior embitters his brothers further. He has two dreams, which he shares with his family. In both of them his parents and his brothers all bend down before him to pay him homage. His brothers are incensed by this pomposity and seek an opportunity to get their revenge. It presents itself when Jacob sends Joseph to check on the condition of his brothers and the flocks they are tending. He is told to bring a report back to his father. There he is, the "master dreamer" (37:19), the favored son dressed in the coat that trumpets the extrava- gance of their father's partiality. Rather than join his brothers in their shepherding, he comes to check on them. Their rage overcomes them, and they devise a plan to kill him and tell their father that his death was caused by a wild animal.

The brothers' plans change when they come upon a caravan traveling to Egypt (37:25). They decide to sell Joseph. In that way they will be rid of him without soiling their hands with his blood. They return to their father with the bloodied coat of their brother and the story that a wild animal devoured him. Jacob is heartbroken; the brothers are free of the troublesome lad; and the first Israelite goes down to Egypt.

In the midst of the collection of traditions about Joseph, we find a very interesting story about the relationship between Jacob's son Judah and Tamar, Judah's daughter-in-law (Gen 38). Judah arranges a marriage between his son Er and Tamar. When Er dies without leaving an heir, Tamar is given to his brother Onan, who also dies childless. Deaths that occurred without leaving children were disastrous for both the deceased man and his widow. Without an heir, a man's name would die with him, and the legal rights to his inheritance could be in question. As for the widow, her future would also be in jeopardy. She would be of no value to the family of her dead husband, so she would probably return to her father's house. There she could hardly be given as a virgin in marriage and would most likely remain as a burden to her family of origin.

To remedy such a situation, the practice of levirate was established. It directed the brother of the deceased to take the widow as his own wife, but the child born of that union would be the legal heir of the deceased brother. This guaranteed the preservation of the name of the deceased, the security of his inheritance within his own family, and the protected station of his widow. The unfolding of the levirate practice can be seen in this narrative about Judah and Tamar.

After the death of his second son, Judah is not willing to offer Tamar his third son, thus reneging on his responsibility to both his first son and his widowed daughter-in-law. Therefore, Tamar takes matters into her own hands (38:14-29). She disguises herself as a harlot and tricks her father-in-law into having intercourse with her. When she is found to be with child, Judah plans to have her burned in punishment for what he believes is an act of harlotry. When Tamar provides proof that it was Judah himself who impregnated her, he relents and acknowledges, "She is more in the right than I am" (38:26). Tamar actually gives birth to twins. One of them, Perez, will be an ancestor of the great king David (see Ruth 4:18-22).

The exploits of Joseph in Egypt read like a fast-moving novel (chs. 39–41). In episode after episode, he is in situations that threaten his life, but he somehow always manages to be saved just in the nick of time, as was the case with the initial betrayal of his brothers. Though a slave, he becomes a personal attendant of Potiphar, a high-ranking official. When he rebuffs the advances of Potiphar's wife, she turns on him, accuses him of sexual impropriety, and prevails upon her husband to imprison him (39:20). While Joseph was in prison, the very ability that earlier infuriated his brothers now serves him well. His talent for interpreting dreams brings him to the attention of the pharaoh, who himself is plagued by unsettling dreams. Joseph is called in to explain the dreams to the pharaoh.

Two of the pharaoh's dreams foretell seven years of abundance followed by seven years of want. Joseph's interpretation so impresses the pharaoh that he places Joseph in charge of collecting and storing the fruits of abundance during the time of plenty so that the people will have a supply to rely on during the years of famine. Now Joseph's reading of dreams is put to the service of others rather than to his self-aggrandizement, as was the case in the past. Joseph the slave has now become the second most important man in Egypt.

The famine affects not only Egypt but the neighboring countries as well. Back in the land of promise, Jacob hears of the distribution of food that has been established by Joseph. Without knowing that this man is his long-lost son, he sends the brothers who had betrayed Joseph to Egypt to procure needed food (chs. 42–44). When they appear before Joseph, he recognizes them, though they do not recognize him. After all, he has taken on the look and manner of an Egyptian.

Before giving them food, Joseph puts them to a test in order to ascertain whether or not they have changed. Under the ruse of holding them as suspected spies, he requires that all but one of them return to Jacob and then bring back to Egypt Benjamin, the second son of his own mother, Rachel. The brothers are struck with terror. They believe that this frightful situation is punishment for their cruelty to Joseph. Though they dearly love their younger brother, they have no choice but to follow Joseph's directions. Jacob is distraught when he hears the conditions set down by the Egyptian who in reality is his son. He is afraid that he might lose yet another beloved son. His family is in need of food, though, and so he acquiesces. Thus Benjamin embarks with his brothers on the journey back to Egypt.

Joseph puts his brothers to a second test. When they are ready to leave Egypt after the second visit, he hides a silver goblet and some money in Benjamin's bags. He then sends men out to apprehend them, claiming that a robbery has taken place. When the brothers who plotted against him come to the defense of Benjamin, Joseph knows that they have indeed reformed, and so he reveals his true identity to them. Joseph's words show that he holds no animosity toward his brothers: "It was really for the sake of saving lives that God sent me here ahead of you" (45:5).

This story is a second extraordinary example of reconciliation. Joseph is like Esau before him. Both men were victims of the malice of close kin. Then even before the perpetrators can express repentance, the victims forgive them, thus initiating reconciliation. Joseph is eventually reunited with his jubilant father. Jacob and all his wives and children and possessions are then invited to settle in Egypt, an invitation they accept. This explains how the Israelites came to be living in this foreign land.

The account of Jacob's testament (ch. 49) is more than a story of an old man's blessing of his children. The dying patriarch succinctly characterizes each of his sons. This poem, which was probably composed long after Jacob's death, is really a historical description of the tribe that carries the name of the son. There is no mention of the promise of descendants in this blessing. Jacob and his family have become a vast multitude, so that promise has been fulfilled. Although they are securely settled in the land of Goshen, they are not in the land of promise. The story of the ancestors comes to completion with this aspect of God's promise still unresolved.

It is very difficult to decide on an exact date for the time of the ancestors. Many commentators believe that it was the latter part of the Middle Bronze Age (2000–1700 B.C.). They come to this conclusion from what they know about the migration of Asiatic nations around this time, as well as the later appearance of names similar to those found in these biblical stories. The stories as they have come down to us, however, are credited to the Yahwistic or Elohistic traditions, theological perspectives that have interpreted earlier stories in ways that contain a later additional meaning.

CHAPTER TWO

Out of Egypt

Settled in Egypt

Famine brought Jacob and his wives and his sons and their wives and children to Egypt. Joseph's prominence in the land enabled him to settle his family in Goshen, an area in the northeast delta of the Nile River (Gen 45:10). At that time "the Israelites became so numerous and strong that the land was filled with them" (Exod 1:7). This description of their increase is reminiscent of God's blessing pronounced at the time of creation and again after the waters of the flood receded: "Be fertile and multiply, fill the earth" (Gen 1:28; 9:7). The Bible does not tell us how long the Israelites resided in peace and prosperity in Goshen. At least one generation passed because the story no longer refers to the sons of Jacob themselves. One exception to this is the report of the age of Levi at his death (Exod 6:16). Any further mention of them is a reference to the tribe that bears the respective name.

The story states that a new king came into power, one who did not know Joseph. He turned against the Israelites and made their lives in Egypt unbearable. A brief look at the history of Egypt can provide some background for these events. Sometime during the Middle Bronze Age (2000–1550 B.C.), Asiatic immigrants called Hyksos settled in the northeast delta of the Nile River. "Hyksos" is an Egyptian word meaning "foreign rulers." They established their capital at Avaris, from where they ruled Egypt for more than a hundred years, establishing the Fifteenth and Sixteenth Dynasties of rule of that nation. A successful uprising against them originated in Thebes, which became the capital of Egypt until the rule of Amenotep IV (also known by the Greek name Amenophis IV). This pharaoh, who ruled in the middle of the Late Bronze Age (1550–1200 B.C.), during the Eighteenth Egyptian Dynasty, inaugurated a religious reform that suppressed worship of all gods but Aton, the sun disc. Temples were closed, and religious personnel were deprived of their livelihood and stripped of their authority. The financial influence of the temple system was shattered, and the nation experienced economic crisis.

This pharaoh changed his name to Akhenaton ("servant of Aton"). He made Akhetaton (also known as Amarna) his capital, and he ruled from there with his wife, the famous Egyptian beauty Nefertiti. Akhenaton's attempt at a kind of monotheism lasted less than two decades. It was certainly not a true monotheism, for Akhenaton himself attained semi-divine status. Under the reign of Tutankhamen, his successor, this renegade religion was suppressed, the temple of Aton was destroyed, foreign influences were crushed, and the old religious practices devoted to the traditional gods of Egypt were reinstated. When Tell-Amarna was excavated, letters from Canaanite kings were unearthed, revealing both the Egyptian control of Canaan and the political chaos that existed there. While some minor kings remained loyal to the pharaoh, the leaders of other tribes vied for power. To further complicate this situation, nomadic people called Hapiru were fomenting unrest.

This short sketch of Egyptian history reveals several details resembling features that we find in the biblical account of the Israelites in Egypt. First, it is clear that there was indeed a time in Egypt's history when it was overrun by Semitic people, who gained significant power in the land. Second, Egypt did indeed experience a religious reform that introduced, if only for a short time, the worship of one god. Third, when a new pharaoh ascended the throne of Egypt, he suppressed this religious movement and attempted to remove all threatening foreign influence from the land. Finally, an upheaval occurred in the land of Canaan, and one of the threats to Egyptian control of that area was an army of marauders called Hapiru.

Although the Egyptian and the biblical accounts demonstrate several similarities, the dates ascribed to the events in Egyptian history do not correspond to what is known of Israelite history. Therefore, we cannot identify the Israelites with the people referred to in Egyptian chronicles. Still, the outlines of that ancient history provide a background for understanding the events described in the Bible. In other words, the story of Israel's origins is not fabricated; it is a reinterpretation of known historical traditions.

The oppression that the Israelites suffered in the land of Egypt is described as slave labor. Their participation in the building of the great pyramids for which Egypt is so well known was indirect. They do not seem to have labored on the great structures themselves, but on two of the major Egyptian supply cities. We see in the first chapter of the Book of Exodus that God's promise that they would be a great nation was being fulfilled: "They became so numerous and strong that the land was filled with them" (Exod 1:7), so much so that the pharaoh sought to curb their increase by issuing a decree that all male babies were to be killed.

Although midwives did what they could to save them, the lives of these infants continued to be in danger. English versions suggest that the midwives were themselves Israelites, but the Hebrew text can be translated "midwives to the Hebrew women." This would mean that non-Israelite women conspired against the ruling of the pharaoh and saved Hebrew babies. This view is reinforced by a claim that Hebrew women would be unlikely to make to the pharaoh: "The Hebrew women are not like the Egyptian women. They are robust and give birth before the midwife arrives" (Exod 1:19). Concern of the non-Israelite women is also seen in the behavior of the pharaoh's own daughter and her maid. They know that the child in the basket is Hebrew, and they save him nonetheless (2:6). Throughout all of their anguish, the Israelites did not cease to call out to God for relief. The stage is set for the drama of God's deliverance of the Israelite people (2:2-25).

Moses

It is through the leadership of Moses that God delivers the oppressed Israelites. Before he participates in the salvation of his people, Moses himself is saved twice. He is first saved by his mother, who places him in a basket by the river, with his sister keeping watch over the basket (2:3). He is then saved by the pharaoh's daughter, who has him drawn out of the water, adopts him as her own, and names him Moses. Some commentators argue that this name comes from the Hebrew for "to draw out." Others insist that it is of Egyptian origin, found in many Egyptian names such as Tutmoses, meaning "born of." The name may have Israelite links, but the story says that Moses was raised in the household of Pharaoh. Therefore, his must have been an Egyptian name.

The tradition does not say when Moses learned of his Israelite ancestry. It does say that he is appalled by the treatment under which the people to whom he belongs are forced to labor. Seized with rage, he strikes and kills an Egyptian overseer, an act that places his own life in peril. He flees Egypt and finds refuge with the Midianites, a tribe that at various times inhabited the Transjordan (the land east of the Jordan River) or territory in the southern part of the land of Canaan. Some commentators believe that these people were a Hyksos tribe; others maintain that they traced their ancestry back to Abraham through his wife Keturah (Gen 25:4).

Moses takes a wife, who is the daughter of a priest of Midian, and they have a son named Gershon, which means "I am a stranger in a foreign land" (Exod 2:22). In one passage the father-in-law of Moses is named Reuel (2:18); in another it is Jethro (3:1). This is an instance where two traditions have been woven into one. The story of Moses meeting his future wife at a well where she comes to draw water (2:16) is reminiscent of the stories of Rebekah and Rachel, who also went to wells for water and found their future husbands there (Gen 24:15; 29:10).

The account of God's self-revelation to Moses is striking. While tending the flock of his father-in-law, Moses comes upon a bush that is burning yet not consumed. As he approaches this wonder, God speaks to him from the midst of the bush, identifying the place as sacred ground and telling him that the cry of the oppressed Israelites has been heard. In fact, he, Moses, has been chosen by God to lead the people out of the land of bondage into the land promised to their ancestors (Exod 3:7-8). It was at this time that God's personal name was revealed (see p. 2).

Moses objects to the role that is outlined for him and insists that he does not have the necessary oratorical skills to perform the task. God counters this claim by assigning his brother Aaron to speak on his behalf. This explains why Aaron will accompany Moses to deliver God's message to the pharaoh. So Moses takes his wife and family and returns to Egypt and to his suffering kinfolk. On the way he meets Aaron and tells him of God's plan for them. Together they approach the elders of Israel, assuring them that God has heard their cry for help and explaining how God intends to deliver them from their servitude.

Pharaoh's obstinacy is countered by a series of plagues that show the power of the God who is demanding that the Israelites be set free. The plagues themselves may have been natural phenomena that occurred at times in Egypt, but the biblical writer saw them as signs and wonders of the power of the God of Israel. The number of plagues varies in different traditions. Only seven are listed in the psalms (Pss 78:43-51; 105:26-36), while the Exodus tradition lists and describes ten (7:14–11:10).

The plagues are more than simply punishment for Pharaoh's sinfulness; they demonstrate God's extraordinary power in two principal ways. First, they show that the God of Israel rivals the gods of Egypt, exercising power outside the land of Israel, in the land under the jurisdiction of the Egyptian gods. Second, although the Egyptian magicians are able to match some of the first wonders performed by Moses and Aaron, their inability to match the more spectacular marvels shows that Israel's God is mightier than the power of the Egyptian gods. The events demonstrate the indisputable might of the God of Israel.

Each time Pharaoh acknowledges his sinfulness, the natural disaster that had befallen is ended. But when he sees that his land and his people are no longer plagued by the phenomenon, he becomes obdurate again. His behavior precipitates the tenth, final, and most devastating plague—the death of the firstborn (Exod 11). This tragedy is momentous for several reasons. The firstborn of both humans and animals was considered the promise of the future. It symbolized fertility and great increase. To strike down the firstborn was to extinguish this hope of a future. In particular, a firstborn son carried into the future the name and, therefore, part of the essence of his father. He was the heir in whose safekeeping the inheritance of the family was entrusted. His death shattered the fabric of patriarchal kinship patterns.

The story of the slaughter of the firstborn of Egypt and of the subsequent departure of the people of Israel reflects elements of an ancient nomadic herding ritual. Before herders embarked on the move from one pasturage to another, they frequently offered a sacrifice to a night demon to protect them from the dangers of night travel. They would offer a young lamb and sprinkle its blood on the doors of their huts or the flaps of their tents. They then felt secure to launch out into unfamiliar territory. This rite became the format of the ritual found in the biblical text. There we see that it is not a night demon but the LORD who moves through the camp, passing over all those dwellings marked with blood. This blood is life-saving for the Israelites, but death-dealing for those who fail to mark their homes with it. The Israelites are not merely moving out in search of new grazing land; they are moving toward a land promised them by their God.

The sacrifice itself is replete with meaningful ritual details. Calendric features (tenth day of the first month) are given to ensure appropriate future commemoration. The lamb must be a year old, approaching maturity, with all the potential that this suggests. It should be unblemished because only what is flawless is worthy to be offered to God. It should be male because a flock can afford to lose a male animal but not a female one, which carries great potential of fertility. It must be slaughtered at twilight, the time when the new day begins (in Jewish custom day begins when one can see the first three stars in the evening sky). Whatever is not eaten is to be burned because this sacrifice is a kind of holocaust. Regulations for the people's attire are also given. Here, too, urgency is behind the directive to dress as if in flight.

Just as there was an earlier ceremony behind the sacrifice of the lamb, so there was an agricultural festival behind the practice of eating unleavened bread. At the beginning of the barley harvest, only bread made of the new grain was eaten. It was prepared without leaven or yeast, which was a fermenting agent and symbolized what was decaying. The bread eaten at the time of the LORD's passing-over is to be unleavened because the urgency of the departure of the people will not allow for the time needed for yeast to ferment. Furthermore, they are embarking on a journey that will take them to a new place. Therefore, they should not partake of anything of the old.

In this account and in the yearly memorial celebration that will commemorate Israel's freedom from bondage, these two ancient festivals are brought together. A third dimension of this ritual is found in the injunction to repeat it. The people are told to "celebrate this day throughout your generations as a perpetual institution" (12:17). Here we see how ancient nomadic and agricultural rituals are infused with new religious significance, and then this newly instituted ritual is given historical meaning that will be remembered down through the centuries.

Signs and wonders

The account of the crossing through the sea (14:10-31) is not only a story of great suspense and drama, but it is rich in mythological symbolism as well. It reflects the cosmic drama of creation found in the Mesopotamian epic *Enuma Elish,* in which a young warrior-god slays the monster of chaotic waters, cutting her in half. In the Israelite story of the exodus from Egypt, the waters are separated by the God of Israel and secured safely on opposite sides, allowing the people to cross through these walls on dry land. As was the case with the blood of the sacrificed lamb offered the evening before this incident, the water that is life-giving for the Israelites is death-dealing for the Egyptians.

From the point of view of history, this is an account of the liberation of an oppressed people, but there is another dimension to the story. Through the power of God who is leading them, this people passes through chaos and arrives on the other side as a new creation, a liberated people. This notion of being freed becomes the core of their national identity. They are not merely the chosen people, descendants of Abraham; they are now also the people whom God liberated with "a mighty hand and an outstretched arm" (Deut 4:34; 5:15; 7:19; 11:2; 26:8; Ps 126:12; etc.). Their God is certainly a warrior, able to vanquish the forces of Pharaoh, considered by some to be a god. The way this story is told shows that Israel believed that its national patron-god, the one who rescued them from the powers of Egypt, was none other than the God who conquered the cosmic forces of chaos at the time of creation. This can be clearly seen in several of the psalms (Pss 24; 74; 77; 95).

The hymn that Moses and the people sing after participating in this marvelous deliverance, referred to as the Song of the Sea (Exod 15:1-21), is considered by many scholars to be one of the oldest sections of the entire Bible. In it God is praised for having raised a storm to overthrow the forces of Egypt. Ancient Canaanite myths portray the major god of their pantheon as a storm deity, raging through the heavens, riding on the clouds, with lightning rods as arrows in his quiver. Israel appropriated this myth and then characterized its God as the undisputed deity, exercising sole control over the forces of nature. Here again we see the image of the cosmic warrior in control of all of the powers of heaven.

This song in praise of God originated long after the events that it celebrates, for it also describes the people's entrance into the land of promise (15:13-18). The lands that are mentioned in the song are Israel's neighbors. Philistia is the territory that runs north and south along the Mediterranean Sea, east of Canaan. Edom is the region west of the Negev desert, southwest of the Jordan River. Moab lies just north of Edom. Canaan is the land that Israel will claim as its own, promised to them by their God. These are the stretches of land through which the freed people will pass and in which they will ultimately settle. This hymn describes the fear that the inhabitants of these lands will experience as they realize that the release of the Israelites actually threatens their own security.

Besides the plagues and the miracle of the seas, God performed signs and wonders while the people were in the wilderness. Chief among these were the phenomenon of the manna, the spectacle of the quail, and the miracle of water from the rock. These marvels demonstrate not only God's provident care but also God's enduring patience. They are God's loving response to the people's dissatisfied complaints. As difficult as it may be to imagine, despite having been delivered from Egypt by means of remarkable signs and wonders and protected against the chaotic waters, the people murmur against Moses. The steadfastness of this people is suspect, and therefore God puts them through a series of tests (15:25; 16:4; 20:20), offering them opportunities to demonstrate their loyalty. Each time they fail miserably. The first test takes place after they come upon water that is bitter to the taste. They grumble, but eventually they find springs of fresh water, near which they camp (15:22-27). As they enter the desert of Sin (known today as the Negev), they grumble about food, and God provides them with quail and manna.

The quail that the wanderers caught and ate may have been small migratory birds that follow the wind. If the wind shifted, exhaustion often forced these birds to land, making them easy prey for hunters of any kind. The manna that appeared on the desert floor was probably a sweet substance exuded from the tamarisk tree. When it dried, it turned to flakes and was sweet to the taste. The substance of which it was made prevented it from being stored, so it had to be collected daily. The name "manna" comes from the question asked by the Israelites when they first saw this unfamiliar phenomenon: "What is this?"— *man hú* (16:15). A second version of these events is found in the Book of Numbers (Num 11:4-9, 31-34). The duplication shows once again that more than one tradition is behind the final form of the story.

Perhaps the most spectacular event that occurred in the wilderness was the theophany, or divine manifestation, that took place on the mountain. Though this mountain has come to be known as Sinai, the account in the Book of Exodus indicates that that name really belongs to the desert in which the mountain is located (19:1). In other places in the Bible, this mountain is named Horeb (Exod 3:1; Deut 9:8; 29:1; Ps 106:19). The description of the event that occurred contains several ritual features, suggesting that the story is more a liturgical explanation than a precise historical account. These ritual characteristics include calendric identification (the first day of the third month, the third day after arrival); a dense cloud, such as was common at shrines whenever burnt sacrifice was offered; personal sanctification and the washing of clothing (requirements of the purity code—Lev 17:15); limited access to the mountain on which God is present; and trumpet blasts. Most likely, as the people commemorated an extraordinary experience of God that took place in their past, elements of their liturgical commemoration were incorporated into the original story. As that story has been handed down to us, it is now very difficult to separate the original story from its liturgical enhancement.

Israel believed that the encounter with God on the mountain was the event that really constituted them as a people. It was here that God promised them: "You shall be my special possession, dearer to me than all other people, though all the earth is mine. You shall be to me a kingdom of priests, a holy nation" (Exod 19:5-6).

Several aspects of this promise merit a closer look. It is from the phrase "dearer to me than all other people" that the idea of "chosen people" is derived. This reflects an ancient belief that each people had its own patron-god who protected them and to whom they owed allegiance. The God who brought Israel out of bondage in Egypt and who communicated with them from this mountain was Israel's God, and they were this God's people.

"Kingdom of priests" and "holy nation" point to the religious character of this people. Since priests were traditionally set apart to perform sacred duties, this designation implies that the entire nation would have this responsibility. In the religion of Israel, holiness pertains to the qualifications needed to participate in worship, not to the moral character or piety of the person. Therefore, the passage suggests that Israel, as God's chosen people, is set apart for allegiance to this mighty God. And how will the people fulfill this weighty responsibility? It will be accomplished through fidelity to the covenant that God is making with them (19:5).

The covenant

The laws which Israel cherished and which are found in the Bible can only be properly understood if they are placed within the context of the covenant. They are certainly a part of this contract, a very significant part, but they are only a part. The most important facet in this complex of theological beliefs is the concept of covenant itself. This was a common ancient Near Eastern legal agreement made between gods and those devoted to them, or between kings and their subjects. There were also parity covenants between equals (Gen 26:28). Some pacts were conditional; others were unconditional (Gen 15:18). Examples of all these types can be found in various places throughout the biblical text.

The covenant made at Sinai was a conditional covenant, inaugurated by God and requiring something from the human partners. It reflects the pattern of a suzerainty treaty found in ancient Hittite documents. In that kind of contract, a suzerain, or sovereign ruler, entered into covenant with vassals. The suzerainty treaty had six chief characteristics: (1) a preamble, in which the suzerain identified himself (there is no evidence that such treaties were made with goddesses); (2) a historical recital of past benefits bestowed on the vassals by the suzerain; (3) a list of the stipulations now placed on the vassals; (4) a list of the blessings that will ensue from obedience to these stipulations, and punishments that will follow disobedience; (5) identification of the deities who witnessed the covenant-making; (6) provisions for deposit of a copy of the covenant to be brought out and read whenever the covenant is renewed.

It appears that the ancient Israelites were acquainted with this kind of contract, for all these covenant characteristics can be found somewhere within the biblical text. Several, but not all, of them actually follow in sequence in the account of the theophany on Mount Sinai. A brief look will demonstrate this. The preamble can be found in the very first words: "I, the LORD, am your God" (20:2a). This is followed by a short historical recital, which states the core of the people's experience of God: "who brought you out of the land of Egypt, that place of slavery" (20:2b). The covenant stipulations begin, "You shall not have other gods besides me," and continue through the Books of Exodus, Leviticus, Numbers, and into Deuteronomy. The blessings or punishments that flow from obedience or violation of the commandments do not follow the collections of laws contained in these books, but they are found elsewhere in the biblical text. Some of the weightier sanctions have been gathered together in two places (Lev 26; Deut 27–28).

There is evidence that Israel gravitated toward other gods and actually participated in their cults until after the Exile (Hos 2:7; Jer 7:18), but no other deities were ever called upon to witness to the covenant that bound this people to their patron-God. That is not to say that witnesses were not called; those witnesses were simply not considered deities. For example, Joshua set up a stone as a witness to, or a memorial of, the covenant made upon the people's entrance into the land of promise (Josh 24:27). Finally, a directive to renew the covenant and to read the law during this time is found in Deuteronomy (31:9-13). A number of narratives show that Israel did indeed follow this directive (Josh 24:16-28).

The Law

An erroneous understanding of the place of the Law in the religion of Israel influences the way many Christians today judge that Law and the people who prized it. There are several reasons for this misunderstanding. Most prominent among them might be the way Paul in his writings criticizes strict observance of that Law as a guarantee of salvation. It is important to remember that his appraisal of the Law is part of the way he argues that Jesus alone is the source of salvation. Furthermore, we must take into consideration the character of his audience. When he is speaking to Gentiles who do not have a strong tradition of a law revealed by God, he says very little about observance. When his audience is observant Jews, religious people whose cherished tradition insisted that they are God's chosen people called to testify to the world the uniqueness of their God, and to realize their call through the manner of their lives and their worship, he challenges their belief that obedience to the Law will save them. Paul never criticizes the Law itself. He himself was an observant Jew. Rather, he challenges the priorities of his co-religionists. They put obedience to the Law above everything else, while Paul insists that faith in Jesus should be given pride of place.

Another reason why some think that the tradition of Israel is overburdened with law is the literary organization of the Bible itself. All the major collections of law have been gathered together in the Books of Exodus through Deuteronomy. Many readers find this heavy concentration disconcerting. The biblical text could lead one to conclude that all these laws were delivered at the same time. Those who misunderstand the organization of the material may not realize that various laws originated at different periods in Israel's history, were collected much later, were arranged according to theological perspective, and were then placed in the narrative that recounts God's entrusting the Law to Moses. Such people may be unfamiliar with the way ancient people established religious legitimation for their traditions. At that time this was often accomplished quite simply. Statutes enacted centuries after the time of Moses were granted Mosaic legitimation when they were linked with earlier law codes that were already credited to Moses.

Finally, the character of some of the laws troubles countless readers. Many of the laws betray extraordinary bias against women; they demonstrate undue concern for physical suitability; and they pay inordinate attention to cultic details. Without excusing the clear bias against women, we should remember that these laws enshrine the values and concerns of an ancient society that was patriarchal (father-headed) in structure and androcentric (male-centered) in perspective. We should not be surprised if they reflect such bias. The concern for physical suitability springs from the desire to offer to God only what is physically intact and in conformity with the prevailing standard of excellence or perfection. The inordinate attention given to cultic details reveals the importance of appropriate worship in the religious life of the people. Israel's laws regulate social and/or religious customs that are very different from those of contemporary societies. We misunderstand their meaning and we misread their purpose if we judge them according to the customs of our own day.

The laws of the Bible are expressed basically in two ways. Most of them are in casuistic or case form, describing a particular situation in which a social custom or principle is breached and prescribing the punishment that is to be imposed after such violation. The degree of culpability is determined by the circumstances of the case. Any change in circumstance will modify the degree of culpability, and the punishment will be adjusted accordingly (Exod 21:12-14).

The second law form is easily recognized by most people. Called apodictic, this form is expressed as "Thou shalt . . ." or "Thou shalt not . . ." It states situations that are incontestable, often treated as pronouncements of divine authority. Frequently the penalty for violation of this kind of statute is death (see Gen 2:16-17). These law forms and their various penalties provide a glimpse into the ethical standards that governed the lives of the ancient Israelites.

The apodictic law formula is well known because the Decalogue (the Ten Commandments) is written in that form. It contains the basic stipulations of the covenant made between God and the people of Israel, setting the tone and direction of the major codes of law. The Decalogue has come down to us in two versions, one found in the Book of Exodus (20:2-17) and the other in the Book of Deuteronomy (5:6-21). The slight variations in these versions are explained by the different times and places of their origin. The version in Exodus is ascribed to the northern Elohist (E) tradition, while the one in Deuteronomy belongs to the Deuteronomist (D) tradition, which originated in the north but went through several stages of reinterpretation and expansion before it attained its final form at the time of the Exile (532 B.C.).

The Bible contains three major collections or codes of law. The Covenant Code (Exod 20:22–23:19) follows the Decalogue in the Book of Exodus and gives some specific direction as to how that list of commandments is to be observed. It received its name from this placement following the account of the making of the covenant and from a reference in the Bible itself (Exod 24:7). Though primarily casuistic in form, it also includes some apodictic statements. Although it begins with a few short injunctions concerning worship, most of the ordinances found there pertain to social behavior. It is here that we discover Israel's policies regarding slavery and directives for handling issues of personal injury as well as damage to or theft of property. There are social laws that govern the relationships between men and women and religious laws that regulate cultic celebrations. References to houses (22:1), harvests and wine presses (22:28) suggest a society already established and relatively prosperous in the land. This is an example of later laws being incorporated into the account of an earlier experience.

The Covenant Code ends with a brief list of blessings that will be granted for observance of the ordinances. Following this is an account of the ratification of the covenant. Young bulls are sacrificed. Half of their blood is sprinkled on the altar. Before the other half is sprinkled on the people, the book of the covenant is read to the people, and they all respond: "All that the LORD has said, we will heed and do" (24:7). The blood of the sacrifice becomes the blood of the covenant, sealing the bond that joins the two partners—God and the nation of Israel.

The remainder of the Book of Exodus, with one noteworthy exception, consists of cultic directives (chs. 25–31; 35–40). The cultic nature of these regulations has led scholars to ascribe these chapters to the Priestly (P) tradition. Here we find plans for the building of a suitable dwelling for God. Instructions are given for constructing the ark of the covenant, the table on which the showbread will be placed, the lampstand that will be set within the tent, the altar of incense, and the laver. There are prescriptions for the clothing of the priests and the rite for their consecration. The detail characterizing these directives could hardly be the product of a community recently escaped from bondage and now wandering through the wilderness. These ordinances, too, most likely originated at a time when the people had the means to procure the materials prescribed.

This block of cultic law is interrupted by the account of the apostasy of the people and the renewal of the tablets of the Law (chs. 32–34). The inconstancy of the people and the fickleness of Aaron might almost be humorous but for the seriousness of their offense. Since Moses has been absent from them for a long period of time, the people go to Aaron in search of a god who might lead them. Aaron acquiesces to their demands and fashions a molten calf out of their earrings. When Moses finally comes down from the mountain, where he has been communing with God, Aaron explains: "I threw it [the jewelry] into the fire, and this calf came out" (32:24). Three thousand Israelites were slain because of their complicity in this violation of covenant commitment. Aaron, however, was not punished for his part in the apostasy. No reason is given for sparing him. Perhaps it reflects a later editor's reluctance to cast the ancestor of the priests in a bad light.

This story comes from the Elohist (E) tradition. Behind it might be an event that took place in the territory of the north after those tribes seceded from the control of the southern Davidic monarchy (1 Kgs 12:16). At that time Jeroboam, the ruling monarch in the north, set up shrines at the furthest northern and southern boundaries of his kingdom. He hoped that this move would persuade his subjects to worship God within the boundaries of his kingdom rather than travel to the Temple in Jerusalem and risk compromising their allegiance. There is archaeological evidence showing that it was not uncommon at that time to construct pedestals in the form of young bulls, upon which images of gods were placed. Jeroboam may well have set up such pedestals without placing any images on them, since the worship of Israel's God was aniconic (icons or images of God were forbidden). Once the Temple in Jerusalem was considered by many to be the only valid place to worship God, any rival shrine was seen as idolatrous. Reverence shown to the vacant pedestal could easily deteriorate into worship of the pedestal itself. Simply setting up these shrines was deemed by some as a violation of the ordinances regulating worship.

The account reports that the people acclaimed the calf as the God who brought them out of the land of Egypt. In other words, they accorded to a figure fashioned out of their earrings the homage that rightfully belonged to the mighty God who delivered them from bondage. God threatened to destroy these faithless people (32:10), but Moses interceded on their behalf. When Moses came down from the mountain and discovered the extent of their apostasy, he was so enraged that he broke the tablets upon which God had written the Ten Commandments (32:20). He then had the Levites put three thousand people to the sword.

Moses returned to Mount Sinai, where he cut two more tablets with the Law. It is important to note that at this time Moses had another profound experience of God when something about the character of God was revealed to him. The LORD came out of the cloud, stood with Moses, and cried out: "The LORD, the LORD, a merciful and gracious God, slow to anger and rich in kindness and fidelity" (34:6). The mercy and graciousness of God are not revealed because the people are righteous but after they have fallen into apostasy.

The second major collection of laws is known as the Holiness Code (Lev 17–26). It belongs to the Priestly (P) tradition and consists of both social and cultic ordinances, all of which have one principal end in view—the ritual purity of the community. It opens with regulations regarding the sanctuary and sacrifices, and it concludes with a list of blessings and curses. The Israelites believed that life was found in the blood, and so they oversaw the shedding or the natural flow of blood, both human and animal. The importance of kinship relationships can be seen in the strict regulation of sexual behavior stated here. Laws governing social behavior and rubrics for religious celebrations are included.

Israel's holiness tradition expanded beyond the Holiness Code itself. It contained certain terms that carry meanings quite different from those used today: holy, clean, and unclean. All societies have standards by which persons, places, and objects are judged appropriate. These standards are culturally determined and are generated out of some earlier experience. For example, people who are familiar with water animals that have both fins and scales might consider shellfish an anomaly because they do not fit this pattern. Such seafood might be proscribed (Lev 11:9-10). Another example can be found in the classification of land animals. We do not know why Israel forbade the consumption of pork. Perhaps there had been an outbreak of disease related to this animal sometime in their past. Whatever the case may have been, the people were only allowed to eat the flesh of an animal that had cloven hoofs and that chewed its cud (Lev 11:3-6).

Furthermore, bodily fluids belonged within the body, except waste that was regularly eliminated. Any untimely or unseemly emission of bodily fluids or oozing through the skin made that person unclean (Lev 13:1-3). Because of the sacredness of blood, the shedding of it, whether through violence or as menstrual flow, made a person unclean. What fit the ordained pattern was considered clean, what did not fit was deemed unclean. Only what was clean was "holy" enough to be involved in religious ceremonies.

One cannot stress strongly enough that these regulations dealt with ritual suitability, not with moral rectitude. Israel maintained that its God was holy, set apart from all other gods. For this reason, as the special people of this holy God, they too must be holy or set apart from all that is not fitting: "For I, the LORD, am your God; and you shall make and keep yourselves holy, because I am holy" (Lev 11:44). This explains the great emphasis this tradition placed on the cult and its sacrifice, the cult personnel and everything that pertains to them, the liturgical calendar, the Temple and its furnishings.

The notion of contagion flowed from a strict interpretation of ritual purity. If one touched something that was unclean, that person became unclean by contagion (Lev 11:39). This explains why those professions that dealt with dead bodies, such as undertakers or shepherds, were despised. Those in such professions were placed in the state of ritual uncleanness, which prevented them from participating in worship. Though some contagions lasted longer than others, people who placed themselves in such jeopardy were themselves shunned. Because a woman was ritually unclean during her menstrual period and at the time of childbirth, her husband was forbidden to touch her during those times, or he too would become ritually unclean and unable to participate in ritual ceremonies. Though these regulations may seem extreme and discriminatory to us, they reflect Israel's desire to recognize the mystery of life and the powers that govern it, to keep order in the community, and to offer to God only what was fitting.

Wandering

The Hebrew name for what has come to be known as the Book of Numbers is "in the wilderness." This name reflects the geographic context of the stories that comprise the book. This book recounts the movement of the people from Mount Sinai through the wilderness to the plains of Moab just across the Jordan River from the land of promise. The Greek name comes from the census figures with which the book opens. In this book we find the Priestly (P) version of accounts found in Exodus (manna and quail, 11:7-9, 31-34), as well as various stories found in no other place. The Priestly character of this book can be seen in the attention it gives to cultic practices and to the degree of ritual purity required of the people. This strong cultic focus points to the fact that it is possible to observe religious practices outside the land that Israel will call its own.

It is in the Book of Numbers that we find the story of Miriam's and Aaron's jealousy of Moses, and of Miriam's subsequent leprosy as punishment (ch. 12). As was the case with the story of the molten calf (Exod 32), Aaron seems to have escaped without punishment. Might this be another example of early Israel's reluctance to portray in a bad light the one upon whom the official class of priests was founded?

The Book of Numbers also contains the story that explains why only a few people of the generation that escaped from Egypt finally reach the land of promise. While the people are encamped in the desert of Paran, which was part of the Sinai peninsula, south of the Negev desert, Moses sends scouts to reconnoiter the land of Canaan. Upon their return they describe a land flowing with milk and honey and rich with fruit (13:27). They say that the people living there are fierce, and the towns are heavily fortified. Out of fear and a lack of trust in God, the people revolt and decide to return to Egypt, where they would be sure of food. Such a decision does not merely reveal the desperation of the people, but the decision to return to Egypt implies that they prefer the rule of the gods of Egypt over the protection of the God who delivered them. This is the tenth time that the people put God to the test (14:22), and so God sentences them to die in the wilderness and never see the land of promise (14:23). Only Caleb and Joshua are spared this dire sentence.

Deuteronomy

The third code of law is found in the Book of Deuteronomy (chs. 12–26), which name means "second" *(deutero)* and "law" *(nomos)*. The uniqueness of this book deserves special attention. The very first verse of the book identifies its content as the words of Moses spoken to the people who are about to enter the land of promise. Since the people who had actually experienced the signs and wonders performed by God at the time of the Exodus and during the sojourn had died in the wilderness as punishment for their sins (Num 24:20-23), it was necessary for the next generation to be initiated into the covenant.

Some commentators maintain that the literary format of the entire book is patterned after a treaty formula. According to this view, the first chapters consist of the historical review (1:1–4:43). This is followed by the exposition of the Law (4:44–26:19), a statement of rewards and punishments (ch. 28), and provisions for renewal of the covenant and the reading of the Law (31:9-13). Other commentators organize it as a series of addresses by Moses (1:1–4:49; 5:1–11:32; 29:1–30:20). The law code is contained within the second speech. The book ends with Moses' last will and testament and the account of his death.

The Book of Deuteronomy is filled with dynamic accounts and forceful admonitions. However, it also contains three passages that reveal the heart of the book's theological perspective. The first is the Deuteronomist (D) version of the Decalogue (4:6-21). The second passage is the *Shema*, a prayer that has become the official prayer of the Jewish people. It calls Israel to hear, to be open to the self-revelation of God. It is a testimony to belief in the one true God: "The LORD is our God, the LORD alone" (6:4). This is followed by what has come to be known as the Great Commandment: "You shall love the Lord, your God, with all your heart, and with all your soul, and with all your strength" (6:5). The love referred to here is not an emotional reaction. It implies faithful and lasting commitment. In other words, it does not matter how one feels, it matters how faithful one is.

The third passage is part of the complex of laws, but it has significance in its own right. It is one of the oldest creedal statements found in the

Bible (26:5b-9). It recites the guidance of the people by a merciful God. The pronouns move from third-person description to second-person testimonial. This apparent inconsistency is characteristic of liturgical texts that begin with a description of the past event of salvation and then, by means of a shift in language, incorporate the present worshipers into the power of that event.

Moses' deathbed blessing of the tribes (ch. 33) is reminiscent of the scene of Jacob and his sons before he died (Gen 49:2-27). Despite the long tradition that has ascribed the first five books of the Bible to Moses, the account of his death and burial challenge the historical accuracy of that tradition. In the Hebrew tradition these books are referred to as the Torah, or Law. (The Greek name is Pentateuch, meaning "five books"). Since the Law itself is attributed to Moses, it is easy to see why this entire section called Torah might be ascribed to him as well.

At the end of the book the people stand poised on the plains of Moab, ready to venture into the land that God had promised to their ancestors so many years ago.

CHAPTER THREE

Into the Land

Occupying the land

With the Book of Joshua we leave the five books of the Pentateuch and enter the world of the Deuteronomistic History. This section of the Bible includes the Books of Joshua, Judges, 1 and 2 Samuel, and 1 and 2 Kings. It consists of traditions that reflect the history of Israel from the time the people took possession of the land until they were conquered and taken into captivity in Babylon. Though the stories recount events of this historical period, the final form of the history itself comes from a much later time.

The story of ancient Israel's entrance into and settlement in the land of Canaan is really an artificially constructed narrative made up of various and often contradictory accounts. The Book of Joshua paints a picture of a full-scale, three-pronged successful invasion. In this version the people cross the Jordan River, march into the land from the east, and mount three swift campaigns. They conquer the central part of the land first, then an area in the north, and finally the land in the south. There is a ritual dimension to these battles that is most obvious in the account of the battle of Jericho, where the priests march in procession around the city before its walls collapse. In this version of the occupation the Canaanite inhabitants are either driven out of the land or put to death.

The Book of Judges provides a very different picture. It contains stories of limited, fierce Canaanite resistance along with gradual Israelite settlement in the land and integration into local customs. In fact, this second version suggests that it was not until the time of the monarchy that Israel fully occupied the land of Canaan. These discrepancies are evidence of the editor's efforts to incorporate differing traditions into one unified, if uneven, narrative. They also throw into question the notion of Israel's "conquest" of the land.

Scholars have advanced several theories to explain these discrepancies. In developing these theories, they have also relied on information about Canaanite history gleaned from the literature of other ancient Near Eastern civilizations. The oldest theory of occupation is that of military conquest. This is the traditional view, and it arises from a literal reading of the biblical story. It is reinforced by some of the twentieth-century archaeological findings. Scholars who subscribe to this theory rely on archaeological evidence showing that cities such as Lachish (Josh 10:31), Debir (10:38), and Hazor (11:10) were destroyed sometime during the thirteenth century B.C.

The excavation of Jericho shows that that famous city did indeed experience a great conflagration, but this destruction did not take place at the time the biblical account suggests. In fact, the site does not seem to have been occupied from the fourteenth to the ninth centuries, precisely the period when the tribes of Israel would have been moving through the land. No one denies that the Israelite tribes were involved in many violent battles with other tribes and peoples. What is questioned is whether military force was the principal manner of occupying the land and whether their military victories were as decisive as the biblical stories would have us believe.

A second theory of occupation was first advanced during the second half of the twentieth century. It is based on two very different approaches; one is sociological and the other is literary. An examination of the lifestyle of ancient nomadic herders has shown that many of them settled on the edge of seasonal grazing territory, and they eventually became engaged in both herding and agriculture. A closer look at some of the stories of Israel's settlement in the land enables us to recognize them as etiologies rather than historical accounts. An etiology is a creative or imaginative explanation of the origin of something, usually geographic. In the Bible it is often marked by the phrase "to this day" (Josh 4:9; 5:9; 6:25; 7:26; 8:28, 29; 10:27; 13:13; 14:14; 15:63; 16:10). This suggests that while the phenomenon itself may be well known, its deep meaning may have been lost. There are also several etiological place names (Judg 2:5; 6:24; 5:17, 19; 18:12). According to some commentators, texts such as these downplay the historical accuracy of other stories. They require a different way of understanding the biblical accounts, one that recognizes the exaggerated or liturgical character of many of the details. This suggests that Israel's occupation of the land may have been more a gradual settlement and incorporation into the local scene than a swift military conquest.

A third theory suggests that there was a social revolt among the peasants living in Canaan who were under Egyptian control. This theory draws on elements of both the conquest and the infiltration models. From the literary fragments found in the ruins of Amarna (see p. 18), correspondence carried on between tribal kings in Canaan and pharaoh Akhenaton in Egypt during the fourteenth and thirteenth centuries B.C., we know that there was significant unrest in the land of Canaan. We also know that this unrest was either precipitated or aggravated by Semitic marauders called Hapiru, a word that means "outlaw." "Hapiru" sounds very much like Hebrew, a word that is a derivative of the word meaning "to pass over." These "outlaws" were people who had "crossed over."

Those who revolted were probably members of the underclass who lived on the margins of society, burdened by Egyptian taxation and oppressive political city-state organization. Influenced by the outlaws who infiltrated from the desert, the inhabitants threw off the rule of their absent Egyptian overlords and established themselves as independent tribes. Many commentators believe that this semi-nomadic people was a band of refugees from Egypt, who told stories of how their God helped them escape from under Egyptian rule. One can see how the Canaanite peasants and herders, who themselves had suffered Egyptian exploitation, might relate positively to such a story and to the God that it extols.

If this theory is correct, it would mean that the vast majority of the people who eventually comprised the nation of Israel were actually rebellious Canaanites. A passage from a much later prophet reinforces this idea: "By origin and birth you are of the land of Canaan; your father was an Amorite and your mother a Hittite" (Ezek 16:3). This theory of origin in no way nullifies the fundamental tenet of Israelite religion that God delivered them from Egypt. God could just as well have delivered the people from Egyptian rule if they were in the land of Canaan as if they were in the land of Egypt itself. It is deliverance from bondage that is the heart of the matter, not the specificity of the site of that deliverance.

Within the recent past a fourth theory has been proposed. Impressed by the similarity between Israelite and Canaanite artifacts such as tools, pottery, statuary, building construction, etc., found in highland villages, many scholars now believe that withdrawal from Egyptian control was generally peaceful infiltration. This position does not deny the fact that there were some military skirmishes, but it does argue that the primary movement within the land was more a shift in political and eventually religious allegiance than it was the drive of military forces.

This land is your land

Returning to the Bible itself, we discover that the first chapters of the Book of Joshua contain stories of Israel's crossing the Jordan River and entering the land of promise. Before the people venture out of Moab into Canaan, Joshua sends spies ahead to reconnoiter the land. These men encounter a harlot named Rahab, who has heard of God's miraculous rescue of the Israelites in Egypt and is convinced that with such power on their side, her city of Jericho will fall into Israelite hands. Consequently, she actually betrays the people of the city by hiding the spying Israelites. In exchange for keeping them safe, she is promised her own safety and that of her family once the city falls to the invaders.

Rahab is identified as a harlot, and she may well have been engaged in a life of sexual trafficking. The fact that she lives on the outskirts of the city, in a dwelling built right into the wall of the city (Josh 2:15), indicates that she is on the fringes of the community. Her easy access to men further implies that her status within that community is questionable. It should be noted, however, that in strict patriarchal societies, as ancient Israel was, women who fail to conform to social propriety in any way at all are considered harlots. Their non-conformity threatens the gendered structures of society. Rahab might have been living where she was for any number of reasons. What we know for sure is that this woman who lives on the margin of society acts to save an entire group of people who are marginalized.

Several features of the account of the crossing of the river into the land alert us to its liturgical character (3:1-17). First, priests carrying the ark of the covenant lead the entire people out of the camp. The ark was a box two and a half cubits long, a cubit and a half wide, and a cubit and a half high (a cubit was the length of a forearm). It was made of acacia wood and overlaid with pure gold inside and out. There were gold rings on each side through which gold-plated poles of acacia wood were passed so that it could be carried. On the top of the ark was a plate of pure gold with figures of cherubim (angels) fastened at each corner, with wings spread toward the center (Exod 25:10-22; 37:1-9).

The empty center of this cover was believed to be the seat above which the invisible God was enthroned. In this narrative the people are told to observe a distance of two thousand cubits (approximately three thousand feet) from the ark. They are then instructed to sanctify themselves. This entire ritual is reminiscent of the directives observed at the time of the giving of the Law at Mount Sinai (Exod 19:20-24).

The crossing of the Jordan parallels the crossing of the Sea of Reeds at the time of the Exodus. In both cases the waters are miraculously held back, enabling the people to cross on dry land. In this account, twelve stones from the riverbed, representing the twelve tribes, are gathered and set up at Gilgal as a memorial to this crossing (4:8). It is at Gilgal that the Israelite men are circumcised (5:3). It is also there that the people commemorate the Passover during the evening of the fourteenth day of the month. These liturgical details may have been incorporated into the story at a later date when that story was being told during liturgical commemoration of the events. In the retelling of the story and reenactment of the event, current new details might have become part of the traditional story.

The section regarding the end of the manna also contains elements that are uncharacteristic of nomadic conditions. The text says that since the people are now in the land of promise and are able to produce their own bread, there is no need of manna. Therefore, that mysterious bread from heaven ceases to appear. The text mentions "unleavened cakes and parched grain," which the people now eat (5:11). We should remember that the people ate manna in the wilderness because they had nothing with which to make cakes. It seems strange that they are only now coming out of the wilderness, yet they have the necessary ingredients to make cakes. Furthermore, parched grain presumes agriculture and harvest, something that characterizes a much later date. Details such as these suggest that this description of the celebration of Passover is more than a simple historical account. It is quite complex, reflecting several layers of interpretation.

The most obvious liturgical features can be found in the description of the siege of the city of Jericho (Josh 5:13–6:27). The soldiers circle the city for seven days, a liturgical period of time. The ark of the covenant and seven priests accompany them, each carrying a ram's horn *(shofar)*. These are cultic personnel and ceremonial instruments. On the seventh day the priests blow their horns, a signal for all the people to shout, the shout being a liturgical response. The description of the destruction of the city contains a troubling detail called the "ban," which is associated with what has come to be known as the "wars of the LORD." Such wars were thought to flow from the plans and purposes of God. In other words, God not only endorsed them but also actually took part in them, leading the armies into battle and securing victory over the enemies. Because such wars were devoted to God, prayers, sacrifices, and some form of religious ritual often preceded them.

The people believed that since that kind of war was "holy," those who participated in its battles, the camp in which they lived, and the weapons that they used were to be "holy," or set apart, as well. In other words, everyone and everything was to be ritually clean and consecrated to the LORD. Part of this consecration was the "ban." This means that the land was cleansed through the slaughter of the defeated people (Deut 20:16-18). This was considered a way of devoting the city's occupants to God for destruction. The seriousness of this injunction is seen in the punishment meted out for its violation (Josh 7:1, 24-26). As brutal as the slaughter of the people of Jericho may have been, it followed the injunction of the ban.

The second major part of the Book of Joshua reports the division of the land among the tribes (Josh 13–21). In this section the tribe of Judah gets more attention than do all the rest of the tribes. In fact, the further a specific settlement is located from the land assigned to Judah, the less detailed is its description. This suggests that the tradition of land allotment comes to us from the time of the monarchy, when a member of the tribe of Judah exercised power over the entire land. In this account some tribes are given land that lies east of the Jordan River, while others receive land west of it. Certain cities are set aside as cities of asylum, where those guilty of involuntary homicide could find safety from anyone who might seek vengeance. In this tradition Levites (priests) are assigned some cities, with surrounding grazing land taken from territory previously allotted to other tribes. The division of territory and the establishment of certain cities show that the laws of Israel provided for all of its citizens.

The people of the land

Israel did not occupy a land devoid of inhabitants. They seized control from people who were already living there. While their behavior may be troubling to some today, it was quite common among migratory people, as were the Israelites as described in the biblical story. They seem to have found the greatest resistance from the Canaanites, the Ammonites, and the Philistines.

Canaan is the land that Israel believed had been promised to them by God. "Canaanite" is a generic term referring to various groups of people established in the land. They included the Amorites, the Hittites, Perizzites, Jebusites, and Hivites (Josh 11:3). Perhaps the Canaanites were the people already settled in the land when the Israelites entered it from the east, as the biblical story suggests, or perhaps they were disenchanted inhabitants who threw off Egyptian overlordship and joined a small group who came in from the desert to form the nation Israel, as many scholars today maintain.

In any case, the Canaanite worldview and religion threatened the religious life of the Israelites. The Canaanites worshiped many gods and goddesses. They were involved in fertility cults and practiced child sacrifice. The Bible contains evidence that at times Israel, too, engaged in some of these practices. It was this religious threat that the people of God sought to extinguish as they fought to drive the Canaanites out of the land or to put them to death (Josh 3:10). This is not meant to justify their actions, but to explain them.

The Israelite tribes were allotted land on both sides of the Jordan River. One of the kingdoms dwelling in the Transjordan (the eastern side), in the area called Gilead, was Ammon. These people lived in the fertile valley of the Jabbok, a river that flows west into the Jordan. Well practiced in fending off desert raiders, they were able to mount a swift attack on unprepared Israelites. For eighteen years they harassed and oppressed the Israelites before God delivered the chosen people from their hands. The Ammonites were eventually defeated by Jephthah (Judg 11:32).

The Philistines were invading sea people who settled along the southern coastal region of Canaan. The name "Palestine" is actually derived from the word "Philistine." These people established five major cities on the west coast of the land of Canaan south of the major Israelite settlements. Ekron, Ashdod, Ashkelon, Gaza, and Gath made up this confederation of cities. Archaeological findings from these sites indicate that "the Philistines were mighty carousers," as one of the archaeologists commented. This judgment is reinforced by the stories of Samson's involvement with the Philistines (Judg 14:19). In fact, the word "Philistine" has become synonymous with "uncultured" or "boorish."

There was no king in Israel

The short phrase "There was no king in Israel," found in several places in the Book of Judges (17:6; 18:1; 19:1; 21:25), characterizes the political lawlessness in the land of Canaan that marked the period of the Early Iron Age (1200–1050 B.C.). Such a judgment reflects a decidedly pro-monarchy point of view. In other words, the author believed that the tribal league that determined the external organization of the people was failing. The minimal unity that existed among the tribes was inadequate, and a decisive leader was needed to keep order and to force the tribes to fulfill their covenant responsibilities.

Perhaps one of the most disturbing accounts demonstrating the depths of the lawlessness into which the people had fallen is the story of the Levite from Ephraim and his Bethlehemite concubine (Judg 19). In some ways this story resembles the report of the sinfulness of Sodom and Gomorrah. A traveling Levite is granted hospitality in the home of a fellow Ephraimite who lives in the Benjaminite town of Gibeah. When the townsmen demand that the householder hand over his guest, the man offers instead either his own daughter or the Levite's concubine. They take the concubine and abuse her all night long. When the Levite finds her collapsed on the doorstep in the morning, he puts her on his own animal and takes her home. Upon arriving home, he cuts her up into twelve pieces and sends a piece to each of the tribes with the message: "Nothing like this has ever been done or seen from the day the Israelites came up from the land of Egypt to this day. Take note of it, and state what you propose to do" (Judg 19:30). The text states that "all the men of Israel without exception were leagued together against the city [Gibeah]" (Judg 20:11). Once the story is reported, the concubine is no longer mentioned. The contemptible act is referred to as "the crime committed in Israel."

The period of the judges was a time of petty tribal kings as well as individual leaders called judges. Some of these judges were charismatic military commanders who executed the judgment of God on the battlefield. Stories of their exploits are found in the Book of Judges. Very little is known about the so-called minor judges; their role seems to have been more juridical than military.

Information about the military commanders follows a four-point literary pattern that has profound theological significance: (1) The sinfulness of the people incites the wrath of God, (2) which then allows the Israelites to fall prey to one of their enemies. (3) When the people repent of their sin, (4) God raises up a judge who, in the role of military leader, rescues the people from their enemy (Judg 3:7-9). This pattern demonstrates the theory of retribution: Sin brings on punishment; repentance is blessed with salvation.

While this literary/theological pattern may well describe and critique events that occurred during this period of Israelite history, it certainly reflects a theological perspective that arose much later, at the time of the Exile, when the history received its final form (586 B.C.). The first part of the pattern explains why the people suffered defeat at the hands of the Babylonians; the second part encourages the people to repent of their sins so that they might be delivered from their misfortune. This theological pattern is the product of a long and complicated process of theological development and reinterpretation of traditions, not unlike the Yahwist (J) or Elohist (E) reinterpretation of earlier ancestral stories found in Genesis, or the reinterpretation of events that took place while the people were wandering in the wilderness, as narrated in Exodus and Numbers. The pattern of retribution found in the stories of the judges is an example of reinterpretation from the perspective of Deuteronomistic (D) or covenant theology.

Scholars believe that the Deuteronomistic theological perspective developed some time among the northern tribes, as did the Elohist theological point of view. The traditions differ, however, in the material that they reinterpret and the time of their appearance. The Elohist (E) tradition treats ancestral stories and is dated around the ninth century B.C.; the later Deuteronomistic tradition (D) addresses historical material and is postexilic. As we have seen, both traditions include law codes and versions of the Decalogue. While the historical accounts found in the Books of Joshua through 2 Kings probably originated during the times described in those accounts, scholars believe that they were brought together at a much later date. As is the case with all histories, Israel's history was remembered from a particular perspective. For Israel, it was the point of view of covenant fidelity.

A religious reform was initiated during the reign of King Josiah (640–609 B.C.). Renovation of the Temple was part of this reform, and during this time the book of the Law was discovered within its precincts (2 Kgs 22:8). This document then became the blueprint for the reform. Some commentators believe that the book of the Law was a version of the Deuteronomistic History; others hold that the document found in the Temple was simply a version of the Law that then became the lens that influenced the writing of the Deuteronomistic version of history.

Those who maintain that it was a version of Deuteronomistic history suggest that this very first attempt at writing history took place during the reign of King Hezekiah (715–687 B.C.), who also undertook a reform (2 Kgs 18:4-6). Whether they think that one or two versions of history

existed before the Exile, all commentators contend that the final reinterpretation took place during or just after the Exile. The entire enterprise
has come to be known as the Deuteronomistic History because it was a
reading of history from the perspective of covenant theology as found
in the Book of Deuteronomy.

During the time of the judges, before there was a king in Israel, the
tribes were organized in a loose confederation. While they enjoyed
tribal autonomy, they came together at certain times to celebrate religious festivals. There was no central shrine at this time, but the people
did establish some major sanctuaries. The first was Gilgal, a place
between the Jordan River and the city of Jericho. It was here that the
people set up memorial stones to mark their crossing of the Jordan
(Josh 4:20-21); it was here that the men who came out of the wilderness
were circumcised (5:5). This shrine would later play a very important
role in the lives of the prophet Samuel (1 Sam 7:16) and Saul, the first
king of Israel (1 Sam 11:15). Later a second shrine, Shiloh, became the
meeting place for all the tribes (Josh 18:1). The ark of the covenant was
enshrined at Shiloh, and devout Israelites journeyed there to pray
(1 Sam 1:3). The divine military title "LORD of hosts" is associated with
this shrine (1 Sam 1:3; 4:3-4), pointing to its importance during times of
battle. It was from Shiloh that the ark was taken and subsequently lost
in battle (1 Sam 4:11). Shrines were also set up at Ophrah (Judg 6:11)
and Mizpah (Judg 20:1), but they did not play the important roles in the
history of Israel that other shrines did.

The judges

Although the tribal league did not possess strong central authority,
God did raise up strong military leaders called judges, who led the
people through crucial times (Judg 3:9, 15, 31). These judges usually
exercised power only for a short period of time, and their authority
did not extend over all of the people. A few of these judges deserve our
attention.

Deborah is identified as both a prophet and a judge (Judg 4). She exercises juridical authority over the Israelites who come to her for judgment,
and she also wields military authority. As prophet, she summons Barak,
a military commander, and delivers to him the message that she received
from God. Her military significance becomes evident when Barak's refusal to march on the enemy without her compels her to join him on the
battlefield. Deborah is remembered for her determination and leadership
and for the victory song that is attributed to her (Judg 5).

Gideon is known as a reluctant leader (Judg 6–8). When an angel of God appears to him and informs him of God's plan, Gideon demands proof that this is indeed a message from God. The tests to which he puts divine power are almost ludicrous. They are matched only by the farcical requirements God demands of the Israelite army. As the story unfolds, there is no doubt that the victory that ultimately comes really belongs to God.

The story of Jephthah is chilling in its conclusion (Judg 11). The price exacted in his bargaining with God for victory over the Ammonites is the death of his daughter. This story, along with the account of Abraham's willingness to sacrifice his son Isaac, shows that human sacrifice was indeed practiced in ancient Israel. There is, of course, a marked difference in the outcomes of the two stories: the son of promise is spared, while the daughter, an only child, is not.

Perhaps the best-known judge is Samson (Judg 13–16). His story contains details of the classic hero story. As was the case with the major ancestors before him, the birth of this child is miraculous. His mother is barren until an angel appears to her and tells her that she will eventually conceive. She is told to consecrate this child as a nazirite, a name that comes from the Hebrew meaning "to set apart as sacred." Those who were consecrated to God by this vow were bound to abstain from wine and all unclean food, to avoid dead bodies of humans or animals, and to refrain from cutting his hair (Num 6:1-21). Since the child within her is consecrated even before his birth, Samson's mother herself is required to fulfill the nazirite requirements while she carries the child. Samson's military exploits are incredible, but they are all credited to his fidelity to his nazirite consecration.

Samson's love for and marriage to the Philistine woman Delilah is his undoing. She tricks him into revealing the source of his strength, which is his nazirite vow, symbolized by his long hair. When he is tricked and his hair is cut, his bond of consecration is broken. As a consequence, he loses his strength, is blinded by his enemies, and taken captive by the dreaded Philistines. As the story moves toward its conclusion, Samson is finally vindicated. When his hair grows back, his strength returns. He calls upon God to restore his strength. His prayer is answered, and he is able to defeat his captors, but not without sacrificing his own life in the process. This is a thrilling story of commitment to God, human frailty, repentance, and vindication. It is no wonder the Israelites cherished it.

The last judge is Samuel, a man who combined within himself the offices of judge, prophet, and kingmaker. The circumstances that surround his birth are reminiscent of the births of other major characters in the history of ancient Israel (1 Sam 1). Samuel's mother Hannah is barren. One day while at prayer at the shrine at Shiloh, she vows that if God blesses her with a son, she will dedicate him as a perpetual nazirite. Her prayer is answered. She conceives and brings forth a son. When the child is weaned, his father takes him to Shiloh, where he is placed in the service of God under the guidance of the priest Eli.

There is a very human tone to the story of God's call of Samuel. Young Samuel is asleep in the shrine before the ark of the covenant. He hears his name called and mistakes this for a call from Eli. It is only after Samuel is called a third time that Eli realizes that the call is a summons from God. He directs Samuel to answer: "Speak, for your servant is listening" (1 Sam 3:9). The message that Samuel receives is one of doom for the family of Eli. The sinfulness of Eli's sons will prevent them from succeeding Eli in leadership of the people. Samuel will become the religious leader of the people in their stead. Over the years Samuel's reputation as a prophet extends over the entire length of the land, from the territory of Dan in the north to Beer-sheba in the southern desert (1 Sam 3:20). He acts as mediator between God and the people, and he judges Israel as long as he lives (7:15). Finally, it is Samuel who anoints as king first Saul (10:1) and then the glorious king David (16:13).

Charismatic leaders

The judges have been referred to as charismatic leaders. This designation comes from the Greek word *charisma,* or gift, and in this context it implies that the power these leaders exhibit is a gift from God rather than simply natural ability. Several accounts of God's raising up an individual to act as judge state that it is the spirit of the LORD that comes upon him and enables him to perform marvelous deeds. It is this spirit that empowers Othniel to judge (Judg 3:10), that envelops Gideon (Judg 6:34), and that comes upon Jephthah (Judg 11:29).

According to the story, Samson's life is filled with charismatic experiences. The spirit stirs Samson very early in his life (Judg 13:25), empowers him to tear a lion apart (14:6), and to kill thirty men singlehandedly (14:19). It is the spirit that enables him to loosen his bonds and then slay a thousand men with the jawbone of an ass (15:14). The description of these feats may appear to be exaggerated; however, they are said to be realized through the power of the spirit of God, and when the power of God is at work, there is no exaggeration. God does indeed accomplish wondrous works.

The character of this charismatic power should be noted. First and most important is its origin in God. Second, this extraordinary power is intended for the good of the community, not merely for the advantage of the one who wields it. When given to the judges, it is meant to be exercised for the deliverance of the community. Third, this power seems to be only a passing phenomenon, operating within the individual only when it is needed. While this spirit was considered a divine power, it should not be seen as the third Person of the Trinity, a much later Christian concept. Here the spirit is the dynamic power of God that is bestowed on a human being, enabling that person to do extraordinary feats.

The confederation established by the tribes was sacred. The bond that united them with one another was the covenant within which they as a people were joined together to their God. Perhaps the major political responsibility placed upon the members of the confederation was mutual support in times of need. Should one city be under siege from enemies, citizens of neighboring cities promised to come to its aid. The tribes were not always faithful in this regard. In a song sung after a victory over the Canaanite king Jabin, one group is cursed for not coming to help those in need (Judg 5:23). A second story shows that only a strong leader could persuade some of the Israelites to come to the rescue of a city under siege (1 Sam 11:1-7). This reluctance on the part of some of the covenant partners, along with the fact that the people were not confident in religious leadership, precipitated their request for a king.

Ruth

The story of Ruth is found in the Christian Bible between the Books of Judges and Samuel. Most scholars believe that the story itself is fictional, though many details within it describe elements of life as it was lived during the time of the judges. This historical designation is precisely the way the book opens: "Once in the time of the judges there was a famine in the land" (Ruth 1:1). The fact that an Israelite family would migrate back across the Jordan into the land of Moab, and that the sons of that family would marry Moabite women, suggests a date much later than the time described in the story, for during the time of the judges there was no peaceful relationship between these two nations. The story might have been told much later as an argument in favor of establishing a peaceful relationship with other nations. Many scholars ascribe a postexilic date to this short story, along with other similar short stories, such as Esther and Tobit, both of which recount an amicable foreign policy.

While some readers are struck by the love that binds Ruth and Naomi together, a more important dimension of the story is the description of the plight of widowed women in a patriarchal society. In such societies women were under the jurisdiction and protection of their fathers or brothers, and after marriage under that of their husbands or sons. When women in a strict patriarchal society were widowed and childless, they had no legal protector.

Naomi returns to the land of her birth, hoping to find there some kind of assistance from her relatives. Ruth, on the other hand, is not only widowed and childless, but she is a foreigner as well. She has opted to remain with her mother-in-law, despite the discrimination that her status will afford her. These details throw even sharper light on the bond of love that joins the women.

While ancient Israelite custom may not have been attentive to the needs of widowed women, it did provide for the posterity and inheritance of a man who died childless. The levirate law required a male relative of the deceased to take the widow to wife (see the story of Judah and Tamar in Genesis 38). The child born of that union was considered the legal heir of the deceased, entitled to his land and possessions. In this way the name of the deceased would continue down through history, his property would remain within his tribe, and the widow would have a child to care for her in the future.

The story of Ruth hinges on the unfolding of this levirate law. A close relative of Ruth's deceased husband does step forward to claim the inheritance. When he realizes that he will have to take Ruth as his wife and that the inheritance will really go to the child born to her, this relative relinquishes his rights. The custom of taking off one's sandal and handing it to another as a sign of such relinquishment (Ruth 4:7) recalls the birth of Jacob. He was born with a grip on Esau's heel (Gen 25:26), a sign that the one who grasps the heel of another will appropriate the inheritance of that other one, generally the land on which one's heel rests.

When the close relative renounces his rights, Boaz, a more distant relative, steps forward to claim both Ruth and all the holdings that would have belonged to her deceased husband. He is willing to hand over the inheritance when the child comes of age. The child that is eventually born of the union of Boaz and Ruth is the legal heir of Naomi's son, and so Naomi, too, is now assured a place in society.

This is not merely a story of the strong bond between women. It belongs to the family history of David, for the child born will become the father of Jesse, the father of David, who someday will be king. The

Book of Ruth ends with a genealogy that traces David's ancestry back to Perez, one of the twins born of the union of Judah and Tamar (Gen 38:29). It is through Ruth the foreigner that the line of David can be traced back to Judah, who was promised by his father Jacob: "The scepter shall never depart from Judah" (Gen 49:10).

Tribal religion

As mentioned above, a bond that was both political and religious joined the tribes of ancient Israel to one another. Their loose confederacy of tribes was really a theocracy, a form of government in which God is considered the principal ruler. Tribal chiefs were just that—immediate rulers of individual tribes. Judges may have led more than one tribe or city-state, but they commanded military ventures, and their authority endured only as long as the military emergency lasted. From the moment that the tribes entered into a covenant agreement and became a unified association, God was their king.

Furthermore, the law that regulated both the social and the devotional dimensions of their lives was really a religious law. They believed that God had revealed it to them, and they were accountable to God for every regulation. This was the case not only with regard to those laws that pertained to worship but also to laws that governed their communal and social matters. The community members with whom they interacted were also covenant partners of God, and to violate in any way the rights of a covenant partner of God was an affront to God as well.

Religious law regulated every aspect of Israelite life. The people were told what to eat and drink and from what to abstain. They knew with whom they could interact and from whom they should separate themselves. Days began and ended with prayer, Sabbath rest framed weeks, and major events like life and death were marked by sacrifice. The Israelites were, after all, God's people, called into being by God, shaped as a people by God. God directed every step along the way of their journey. They had no meaning outside of God. They were witnesses to the other nations of the world that this God did indeed exist and was, in fact, the only true God. Israel's entire existence was religious to the core.

For the most part, the tribes went about their lives independent of one another. While they did promise military cooperation in times of need, such need arose only periodically. The law required that they meet regularly at major shrines to celebrate agricultural festivals and to commemorate God's active presence in their midst. In this way the entire year was regulated by a religious calendar. Although at different times various sites enjoyed the privilege of being the major shrine, what really determined this privilege was the presence of the ark of the covenant. A copy of the law of the covenant was preserved within the ark (Exod 25:16). It was taken out and read during the ceremony of covenant renewal.

The ark of the covenant was the center of tribal religion. It linked the tribes that were settling in the land with Moses and the people who had gathered at the foot of Mount Sinai. It was the religious symbol of the covenant made in the wilderness. It was the place where God was present in the midst of the people. The people gathered around the ark to worship God (Josh 7:6), and they carried it with them as they marched into battle (6:8-9). In a way, the ark replaced the pillar of cloud that led the people through the wilderness by day and the pillar of fire that guided them at night (Exod 13:21).

There is something to be said about the mobility of the ark. It was not only a symbol of God's presence in the midst of a migratory people, but it also characterized the freedom of this God who was not restricted to one place, as was believed of the gods of other nations. Furthermore, while the ark itself was a tangible object, the God who was enthroned above it was not. The religion of Israel was aniconic, rejecting all icons that might claim to represent God. This feature of its religion set Israel apart from other ancient Near Eastern nations, which represented their gods in various human and animal forms.

The priests became prominent figures at this time because they were responsible for the ceremonies conducted at the shrines. They officiated at the sacrifices and provided the services needed to ensure that the cultic laws of purity were observed. They were also the ones who consulted God in the name of the ordinary believer (Judg 18:6-7). This was accomplished in the following way. The people would come to the shrine in search of divine direction, presenting their concern in a simple question form. The priest would manipulate cultic objects known as the Urim and the Thummim, which could be read in one of two ways, resulting in a yes or no answer (1 Sam 23:9-12). What may sound superstitious to us today was simply a way the ancient people tried to discover God's will for them. A careful examination of their religious practices shows that they believed that their God was an active presence in their everyday lives.

As Israel moved into another form of political organization, its religious thought changed as well. This was because of the religious character of its political and social consciousness and the political implications of its religious beliefs and ritual. This move was not an easy one. No political or religious reorganization is. Such reorganization results in shifts in authority and power, a change in practice and custom, and the need to redefine everything of importance. This was the challenge that faced the Israelite people as they moved closer and closer to a monarchic form of government and further and further away from the tribal confederacy.

CHAPTER FOUR

Long Live the King!

A prophet of the LORD

Samuel is the bridge that connects Israel's tribal organization to a new form of government, namely, a monarchy. The previous chapter included the account of his birth (1 Sam 1:1–3:18); this chapter opens with an acknowledgment of his importance as prophet: "The LORD . . . manifested himself to Samuel at Shiloh through his word, and Samuel spoke to all Israel" (1 Sam 3:21). We have already seen that many of the tribes failed to fulfill the mutual responsibilities that they took upon themselves when they entered into covenant with God and with each other (Judg 5:21). There seems to have been no strong leader who could rally all of the tribes together.

The entire period is characterized by disunity: "There was no king in Israel; everyone did what he thought best" (Judg 17:6; 21:25). Even this statement refers to what appears to be best only for individual tribes or cities, not for the entire people. The people came to realize that if they continued to think only of their own safety and prosperity and not of the safety and prosperity of the entire covenant community, neighboring tribes and nations would be able to defeat them city after city. Their very survival demanded the kind of loyalty that only closer organization might guarantee. It is at this point that we reenter the story.

The symbol of tribal unity is the ark of the covenant, and the site of this unity is the shrine at which the ark is housed. The individual tribes located in the hill country often enjoy natural protection from enemies, and with a certain amount of security and for a period of time, they may be able to thrive independent of other tribes. But they are no match for organized unions of strong city-states such as the Philistines. Israel suffers a particularly shattering defeat at Aphek. Thinking that the presence of the ark of the covenant will guarantee victory, the people petition Hophni and Phineas, the sons of Eli, to bring the ark of the covenant to the battlefield.

At first the Philistines are frightened, for they had heard of the triumph of the God of Israel against the Egyptians. However, the Philistines fight mightily. They defeat the Israelites and eventually capture the ark of the covenant. This is a terrible blow for the Israelites. They not only lose the battle, but they are also stripped of the ark, the symbol of God's presence in their midst. Eli's sons are killed in the battle, and shortly after this Eli himself dies. With no ark, the shrines lose their importance, and with the death of Eli and his sons, there is no priestly leadership. Not only is the tribal union weakened, but tribal religion itself is threatened. Into this scene of defeat and despair steps Samuel.

We have already considered the circumstances that surrounded Samuel's birth (see p. 45). His mother Hannah was barren. While praying at the shrine at Shiloh, she promised to dedicate her child to God as a nazirite if God would only allow her to conceive. Her prayer is answered, and she keeps her promise, bringing the young boy to the shrine, there to serve the LORD under the tutelage of the priest Eli (1 Sam 24–28). As she dedicates her son to God, Hannah cries out in prayer:

> My heart exalts in the LORD,
>   my horn is exalted in my God.
> I have swallowed up my enemies;
>   I rejoice in my victory . . . (1 Sam 2:1).

Inspired by this prayer, a Gospel writer will place a similar prayer on the lips of the young Mary as she rejoices over her own pregnancy:

> My soul proclaims the greatness of the LORD,
>   my spirit rejoices in God my savior . . . (Luke 1:46-55).

This extraordinary birth and the revelation of God to the young boy Samuel regarding the demise of the family of Eli are early indications of his future importance.

Samuel is a transitional figure. Besides acting as a prophet, delivering the word of God to all the people (1 Sam 3:21), he functions as a judge: "It was at Mizpah that Samuel began to judge the Israelites" (7:6), and as a priest, offering sacrifice in the name of the entire people: "Samuel therefore took an unweaned lamb and offered it entire as a holocaust to the LORD" (7:9). Only later when the roles of judge, prophet, and priest become more differentiated will they be assumed by three different groups of people.

Despite the importance of all the roles he played in the lives of the people, Samuel might be best known for his relationships with Israel's first kings. He is the one who identifies and then anoints both Saul, the first king, and then David, Saul's successor. As a prophet or spokesperson of God, Samuel leads the people from their tribal form of government, where God is the undisputed sovereign leader, to a form of monarchy in which, unlike the other monarchies in the ancient Near Eastern world, the human king does not rival the sovereignty of God.

It is important at this point to understand the role of the biblical prophet. Fundamentally, such a prophet was a mediator between God and the people. Besides the prophet, there were other mediators in ancient Israel: seers, diviners, and necromancers, to name but a few. Though there seems to have been very little difference between these functionaries during the time of the judges and the early monarchy (1 Sam 9:9), eventually they became relatively distinct. The seer was someone who looked into the future, much as a fortune-teller might do (9:6); diviners used physical means to discern the future, such as reading the flight of birds, the entrails of an animal, or the way arrows fall to the ground (2 Kgs 13:14-19); necromancers consulted the dead in order to discover the future (2 Sam 28:8). Eventually, these methods of reading the future were condemned (Isa 8:18-19), and only the activity of the prophet as the spokesperson of God was acceptable.

But what was prophecy? The prophet was considered a channel of communication between God and the people. Unlike the seer, the diviner, or the necromancer, who initiated the search for insight into the future, the prophet was the recipient of the word of the LORD in the present. Also, unlike the various forms of divination, it was God who initiated prophecy, not the human functionary. Perhaps the most important character of prophecy was its focus on the present rather than the future. True prophecy was rooted in the responsibilities of the covenant. The character of the people's covenant commitment called forth prophetic activity. Prophets seldom appeared when this commitment was secure and reliable. When the people strayed from their covenant responsibilities or when they doubted God's trustworthiness, prophets arose to condemn their offenses and to call them back to fidelity or to assure them of God's constancy and encourage them to persevere even in the face of difficulty.

When prophets did speak of the future, it was a future envisioned as the consequence of their present decision: if the people were faithful to their covenant responsibilities, they would enjoy God's good pleasure; if they turned away from God, they would experience God's wrath. One could say that true biblical prophecy included aspects of the past, the present, and the future. It was the covenant agreement entered into in the past that directed the way the people were to live in the present so that they would enjoy the fruits of their devotion in the future. Rooted in that covenant, prophecy sought to remedy any disruption of the covenant agreement so that it could continue to thrive.

Although even Samuel identifies himself as a seer (1 Sam 9:19) and after his death participates in necromancy when, at the urging of King Saul, the witch of Endor conjures up his ghost (1 Sam 28:7-11), he is best known as an authentic prophet who communicates God's will regarding the monarchy.

A king to rule them

As already stated, the move from tribal organization was not a smooth or easy one. The tribes chose to attend to their own concerns. They seemed to prefer their autonomy, even though they were in grave need of a leader who could command the loyalty of all tribes. In the ancient world such a leader would be some kind of king. However, at this time kings were generally believed to be direct descendants of gods or to be gods in human form. Thus kings assumed divine status and considered themselves accountable to no one.

Such a situation would be intolerable for Israelites, who maintained that their God was their true sovereign and no human ruler could ever be considered divine. Furthermore, they believed that all Israelites without exception were bound to meet the responsibilities of the covenant. No king could be above the law. We know that Israel did in fact accept a monarchy, but it did so with significant opposition, some of which can be seen in the biblical narratives themselves. Furthermore, when monarchy was finally accepted, it was reshaped to conform to Israelite religious belief.

The elderly Samuel appoints his sons to succeed him. But, as was the case with the priest Eli whom he succeeded, Samuel's sons are not reliable, and so the elders of the people petition him: "Appoint a king over us, as other nations have, to judge us" (1 Sam 8:5). Samuel is displeased with their request and brings it to God. God's response is quite interesting: "Grant the people's every request. It is not you they reject, they are rejecting me as their king" (8:7). Since God agrees to the establishment of the monarch, the passage does grant monarchy divine legitimation. It still represents an anti-monarchy position, though.

The price Israel pays for a monarchy is high. The following delineation of the rights and privileges of the king strikes at the very heart of the people's identity. "He will take your sons . . . He will appoint from among them his commanders . . . He will set them to do his plowing . . . He will use your daughters as ointment-makers . . . He will take the best of your fields . . . he will tithe your crops and your vineyards . . . He will take your male and female servants . . . and you yourselves will become his slaves" (1 Sam 8:11-17). Their boast is that they have been liberated by God to live with relative self-determination.

This passage shows that the monarchy will limit this self-determination. Actually, it is less a prophecy, warning the people of the future, than it is a description of a later monarchy, probably Solomon's, which was read into the story at this point. Samuel's reasons for opposing the monarchy, however, are not devoid of self-interest. After all, he is the prominent religious leader at this time, functioning as priest, judge, and prophet. With a king, he would lose much of his power and influence, and so it is quite possible that Samuel interprets the people's demand as a rejection of his own leadership.

There are passages in the Bible that do reflect a pro-monarchy position. One of them is the account of the selection of the first king, Saul. When the asses of his father wander off, Saul goes in search of Samuel the seer, hoping that the man of God will be able to direct him to the lost herd. Before the arrival of Saul, God reveals to Samuel that he is to anoint the man who will soon visit him. This man will be the "commander of my people" (1 Sam 9:16). Samuel anoints Saul, and tells him that the spirit of God will take possession of him, which it does (10:10). Samuel also cautions Saul to be silent about the anointing until he can be presented before a gathering of all the Israelites. When this was finally done, "all the people shouted, 'Long live the king!'" (10:24).

Though anointed king, Saul functions much more like a judge over all Israel: "After taking over the kingship of Israel, he waged war on all their surrounding enemies" (1 Sam 14:47). He seems to possess the ability to command compliance to his wishes. An incident that occurs early in his reign illustrates this. The Israelite city Jabesh-gilead is under siege from the Ammonites, and Israelite cities that promised to come to its assistance fail to do so. In anger, Saul slays the oxen with which he has just been plowing the field and sends a piece of the flesh to other Israelite cities with the threat: "If anyone does not come out to follow Saul [and Samuel], the same as this will be done to his oxen." The story reports that "the people turned out to a man" (11:7). This is the kind of leader Israel needs—one who can rally the forces, particularly when the people are slow to respond on their own.

Saul begins as king with great promise. God selects him, a mere human being does not; Samuel, the chief religious leader of the time, anoints him, thus giving religious legitimation to his reign. Saul is a very successful military leader, and his victories are seen as evidence of God's good pleasure. Nevertheless, before long he does something that results in his losing favor in the eyes of Samuel, which in Israel's mind was the same as offending God. During one of the military campaigns against the dreaded Philistines, Samuel is slow in coming to the camp to offer sacrifice for the success of the battle. Saul waits seven days, the period of time that Samuel has determined, but still the prophet does not arrive. Realizing that a victory might be lost if they do not move against the enemy, Saul himself offers the sacrifice. When Samuel finally arrives, he berates Saul for his presumption and tells him that this violation will cost him the monarchy. He insists that royal rule will pass over his son and will be given to another (13:2-14). The punishment for an act that appears to respond to military expediency may seem extraordinarily harsh to us. The narrative may simply be an explanation of why the second king of Israel did not come from the family of Saul.

Up to this point the narrative seems to support Saul. The character of the stories now changes. They are increasingly anti-Saul and pro-David. This shift may have less to do with the historical reality than with the political biases of those telling the stories. We see that the relationship between Saul and Samuel deteriorates. This deterioration again means that Saul loses favor with God as well.

Though Samuel grieves over Saul's plight, he is told by God to anoint another king. As with the selection of Saul, the choice for king is God's, not the prophet's or the people's. God directs Samuel to the house of Jesse, a Bethlehemite who has seven sons, one of whom God has already chosen to be the next king. Samuel rejects the six likely candidates and then calls for the youngest son, who is tending the sheep. When David arrives, God reveals to Samuel: "'There—anoint him, for this is he' . . . and from that day on, the spirit of the LORD rushed upon

David" (1 Sam 16:12-13). The last comment explains why both Saul and David are sometimes called charismatic kings. It is because the spirit of God took possession of them.

As soon as David appears on the scene, the character of Saul declines further and further into disrepute. Tormented by an evil spirit, he seeks relief in music. Little does he know that the young man whom he will invite into his camp is the very one who will usurp his throne. Initially David thrives in the presence of Saul. He gains acclaim by defeating Goliath, the giant whom the Philistines sent out to intimidate the Israelites (1 Sam 17:41-51); he befriends and is befriended by Saul's son Jonathan (18:1-5); he marries one of Saul's own daughters (18:27); and he wins the admiration of the Israelite women, who shower him with greater praise for military success than they bestow on Saul himself (18:7).

This latter insult brings back the evil spirit that has been tormenting the king, and from now on David's safety is in jeopardy. Though Saul seeks to kill David, David will not harm the king when he has an opportunity to do so (24:11; 26:9). As the story continues, Saul and David ultimately make their peace (26:17-25), but it is too late for Saul. The die has been cast; the kingdom has been given to David. All that is left is the unfolding of events and the tragic end of Saul.

The friendship between David and Jonathan has been scrutinized and questioned down through the years. Their love was mutual: "Jonathan had become as fond of David as if his life depended on him; he loved him as he loved himself" (1 Sam 18:1); "I grieve for you Jonathan my brother! Most dear have you been to me; more precious have I held love for you than love for women" (2 Sam 1:26). The story itself may have simply been meant to underscore God's choice of David over Saul, a choice that was recognized even by Saul's own son.

The character of the love between these men probably reflects ancient Near Eastern customs. In such cultures marriage to women was frequently an arrangement meant to solidify social or political alliances. The bonds that joined men were often considered as important and lasting as the bond of blood. That Jonathan loved David implies that they were committed to each other; as fellow warriors, they depended upon each other for their very lives. Certainly David would mourn the dissolution of such a bond.

Saul's end takes place at the battle of Gilboa. At this time the armies of Saul cannot hold back the Philistines. They kill Jonathan, the beloved friend of David, along with two other sons of Saul. Even if he had not lost favor with God, now Saul has no strong descendant to succeed him to the throne. Saul himself is seriously wounded during this battle. Rather than be taken alive by his enemies, he asks his armor-bearer to pierce him through with a sword. The man refuses, "so Saul took his own sword and fell upon it" (1 Sam 31:4). When his armor-bearer sees what has happened to the king, he does the same, running a blade through himself (31:5).

There are very few instances of suicide in the Bible. Most of them describe situations where soldiers are suffering mortal wounds and choose this death rather than capture and torture by an enemy. Abimelech (Judg 9:54) and Saul (1 Sam 31:4) are examples of this kind of death. Though they are not mortally wounded, Saul's armor-bearer (1 Sam 31:5) and King Zimri (1 Kgs 16:18) also choose death in the face of military defeat. Samson's story is quite different. He is responsible for his own death, but it took place in the course of his action to kill the accursed Philistines (Judg 16:20). The deaths of Ahithopel and Judas are a completely different matter (2 Sam 17:23; Matt 27:3-5). Their lives are not in immediate jeopardy. They take their lives because they choose not to live with the consequences of the serious mistakes that they have made. Unlike the other deaths, these are genuine suicides.

The story of Saul ends with an episode demonstrating the nobility of David. Faithful to the king to his death, David mourns Saul's death and the deaths of his sons, particularly that of Jonathan, his beloved friend (2 Sam 1:11-12). A second and very different tradition about Saul's death claims that he did not die at his own hand but at the hand of an Amalekite, whom David orders to be killed in retribution for the death of the king (1:15). Though this entire tradition is clearly pro-Davidic, it minimizes the disgrace with which Saul is depicted. In this tradition the man who comes onto the stage of history with such promise departs with less shame than in the earlier version.

The man God raised up

David is considered the greatest king of Israel. He was not only a victorious military champion, but he knew how to win over people and consolidate the fruits of his victories. This point can be seen in the very earliest stories about his exploits. We have already seen that he cleverly outwitted the Philistine giant Goliath (1 Sam 17:41-51); he won over the general populace of Israel with his triumph over their enemies (18:5-7); even after being expelled from the land by Saul, he gained the allegiance of some of the southern Judean cities by distributing among them the spoils he captured from his raids on the Philistines (27:8-12).

It is no wonder that with the death of Saul, the people in Judah move to anoint him as their king (2 Sam 2:4).

Abner, one of Saul's loyal generals, appoints Saul's son Ishbaal to succeed his father as king of the northern tribes of Israel. Thus begins a bitter dispute between Saul's men and David's men. With much intrigue on both sides, this enmity lasts for about two years, until Ishbaal is murdered. The elders from the northern tribes then come to David to implore him to be their king as well (2 Sam 5:2). David is now king of Judah in the south and Israel in the north.

Though a king, David is first a military leader. In this role he captures the Jebusite city of Jerusalem. Judah and Israel ask David to rule over them. Jerusalem, on the other hand, is his city by conquest; he makes this his very own city, the place where he settles his family and sets up his own government. Jerusalem now becomes known as "the city of David" (5:7). It is here that he brings the ark of the covenant (6:17), thus linking the religion of the tribes with a new site of worship. God continues to be in the midst of the people, but God's presence is specifically located in what was formerly a Canaanite stronghold and is now the seat of the monarchy. David now rules over Judah, Israel, and Jerusalem, three political realities originally independent of each other. Though these entities gradually begin to merge, enough difference and animosity remain to result in a breakup after two short generations (1 Kgs 12:16).

We have seen that Saul was explicitly chosen by God to be king, as was David. We will see later that such individual choice will be the primary way the northern kings ascend the throne. Such a method was frequently attended by political conspiracy, social unrest, and extensive bloodshed. The way to avoid the threat of constant upheaval was the establishment of a royal dynasty. Primogeniture, or succession of the firstborn, was already a common practice in the ancient world. The issue here is the designation of the royal family within which such succession would take place. The fact that Saul's son Ishbaal did succeed his father for a time suggests that the followers of Saul's family attempted to establish a Saulide dynasty. We do not know for sure why they were unsuccessful in this effort. Perhaps the answer can be found in the decline of Saul during his final years, along with David's simultaneous rise to power and influence. Whatever the case, a Davidic dynasty was ultimately established, and this dynasty was granted religious legitimation.

From the time he was harassed almost to his death by Saul, David enjoyed the guidance of the prophet Gad (1 Sam 22:5; 2 Sam 24:18). But the prophet most closely associated with this remarkable king is Nathan. He is the one through whom God speaks to David regarding both the construction of the Temple and the establishment of the dynasty (2 Sam 7:8-17); he is the one who accuses David of sin in the death of Uriah and of adultery with Bathsheba and who calls for his repentance (2 Sam 12:1-12); he is the one who conspires with Bathsheba to see that Solomon is appointed the royal heir of David (1 Kgs 1:11-30). It seems that in Israel, behind every great king is a loyal prophet.

Ancient Near Eastern kings were renowned for the expanse of territory over which they ruled, the extent of their wealth, and the magnificence of their buildings, particularly their palaces and temples. Although David was able to capture both the lands and the holdings of weaker neighboring nations and to consolidate the kingdoms of Judah, Israel, and the city-state of Jerusalem, he has not yet made a name for himself as a great builder. The story about his desire to build a temple for God suggests that his motive for wanting to do so was primarily religious (2 Sam 7:2). Whether or not this was the case, the text explains why David never built a magnificent temple, and it is told in such a way as to exonerate him of any culpability in this matter. In fact, the primary focus of the story is on the establishment of the dynasty, not on David's failure to build a temple.

The story clearly states that just as God has been directing the events in David's life from the beginning ("I took you from the pasture . . . I have been with you . . . I have destroyed all your enemies"), so God will be with him in the future ("I will make you famous . . . I will give you rest . . . I will raise up your heir after you . . . I will make his kingdom firm . . . I will be a father to him and he will be a son to me"—2 Sam 7:8-14). Here we see that Israel did indeed appropriate the ancient Near Eastern concept of the king as a son of the deity.

We also see how Israel's monarchy was quite different from the monarchy of its neighboring nations. Israel's kings were first and foremost members of the covenant community like all other Israelites. This meant that they were bound by the Mosaic Law and not above it: "If he does wrong, I will correct him with the rod of men and with human chastisements" (7:14). Despite any sinfulness on the part of the king, however, the dynasty would be secure: "But I will not withdraw my favor from him as I withdrew it from your predecessor Saul, whom I removed from your presence. Your house and your kingdom shall endure forever before me; your throne shall stand firm forever" (7:15-16). Not only is there now a divinely approved Davidic dynasty, but God also guarantees its stability.

The covenant that God made with the Davidic family was quite different from the covenants made with the natural world (Gen 6–9), the one made with the tribe of Abraham (Gen 15 and 17), and the one made with the people at the foot of Mount Sinai (Exod 20). This covenant was exclusive, made only with one Israelite family—the family of David. It was similar, though, to the covenant with Abram that we read of in Genesis 15 insofar as it was unconditional; Abram was required to do nothing. The covenant made with the people at Sinai was a conditional covenant. There were regulations involved, but the people freely accepted the regulations accompanying that solemn pact. These requirements may have been strenuous, but the people freely agreed to them. The covenant with the family of David was predicated on its relationship with the Sinai covenant. In other words, no new regulations were imposed on the royal family, but its peaceful reign was dependent on the king's fidelity to the Law.

The royal tradition that will grow out of these ideas will shape the way the people understand themselves, their kings, and their relationship with God, generation after generation, even down to our own day. It will function as a two-edged sword at the time of the Exile, when the people first doubt God's fidelity to this promise in the face of the conquest of the reigning king, and then cling to the hope that the promise will be fulfilled in the future. It will also be the basis of the royal messianism that will play such an important role in much later Christian theology.

The word "messiah" comes from the Hebrew *māshîah*, which means "anointed one." Originally it referred to any persons who were anointed, such as kings (1 Sam 10:1; 16:13) or priests (Exod 40:13). Dissatisfaction with the leadership of current officeholders led the people to look to the future for leaders who would execute their responsibilities according to God's plan. Gradually hopes for a better future developed into traditions of messianic expectation. The people soon looked to God to intervene on their behalf. They believed that God would send someone who would lead them on the right path.

Throughout ancient Jewish writings we find traces of various messianic traditions. Only a few of them have survived in the Bible: a prophet like Moses was promised (Deut 18:18); Elijah was expected to return before the end of time (Mal 3:23); hopes were placed in the strange figure of one like a "son of man" (Dan 7:14). Such expectations are also found in the New Testament (Matt 16:14; Mark 8:28; Luke 9:19; John 1:21).

David continues to excel as a military leader, adding more and more territory to the land over which he governs. It is during his campaign against the Ammonites that he first sees Bathsheba, the wife of Uriah the Hittite, one of the loyal generals who serves under him. David's desire for the woman knows no bounds, and it leads to adultery. When she informs the king that she is carrying his child, he devises a plan to hide his sin. The innocent Uriah does not comply with David's strategy to have him sleep with his wife (2 Sam 11:11), and so the king takes more drastic steps. Through David's scheming, Uriah dies a hero on the front line, leaving David free to take Uriah's widow as his own wife. The king is not only guilty of personal sin, but he has exploited his political power for his own sinful ends. He has placed the safety of his men in jeopardy in order to cover up his transgression. The prophet Nathan steps forward as God's spokesperson to force the king to recognize his sin (2 Sam 12).

Nathan uses a parable to lead David to see the seriousness of his crime. The king's eyes are opened, and he admits his guilt: "I have sinned against the LORD" (2 Sam 12:13). The punishment of this sin will be felt down through the ages in the dynastic family (12:10-12). The child is stricken. David does public penance in hopes that the child will be spared, but to no avail. The child dies, and David is the first king to feel the sting of the warning made at the time of the establishment of the dynasty: "I will correct him with the rod of men and with human chastisements" (2 Sam 7:14).

A large section of the biblical material that recounts the exploits of David and his sons has come to be referred to as the "Succession Narrative" or "Court History" (2 Sam 9–1 Kgs 2). While it consists of stories that are valuable in their own right, together they also provide an explanation of why Solomon and not one of David's eldest sons succeeded him to the throne. It is here that we find the heartrending story of Absalom, the son whom David loved dearly but who challenged his father's sovereignty and who died in a battle waged against him. David's grief at the death of this son is legendary: "My son Absalom! My son, my son Absalom! If only I had died instead of you, Absalom, my son, my son!" (2 Sam 19:1).

Nathan appears again when David is an old man and the order of royal succession is in doubt. He and Bathsheba conspire to see that Solomon is chosen heir (1 Kgs 1:11-30). Most scholars agree that one of the most influential individuals in the ancient Near Eastern court was the queen mother. She was the one who, as only one of the many harem wives, was able to secure the throne for her son. In appreciation for this, she was granted significant authority and power in her son's court. The present story reflects several elements of this court practice. Here it is clear, though, that it was the prophet Nathan and not Bathsheba who initiated the ruse. Such a ploy would no doubt have guaranteed him a position of importance in Solomon's court.

It is only in the references to the evil spirit that overtook Saul that we read about David's musical ability (1 Sam 16:16-18; 18:10). There is a well-established tradition identifying David as the author of many of the psalms (Pss 3–32, 34–41, 51–65, 68–70, 86, 101, 103, 108–110, 122, 124, 131, 133, 138–145). This tradition probably has less to do with actual authorship as we know it today than with sponsorship. Rather than understanding the Davidic titles of these psalms as identification of authorship, scholars today believe that they indicate the early collection of psalms from which they were taken. (There are also collections ascribed to Temple singers named Korah [Pss 42–49] and Asaph [Pss 73–83].) It is in the reinterpretation of the story of David as we find it in 1 Chronicles that his influence in liturgical practice is elaborated. Although he did not build the Temple, according to this version of his history, he was instrumental in organizing cult singers. While the story recounts David's accomplishments, it is a postexilic description of the organization of the personnel of the second Temple (fifth century B.C.).

Solomon in all his glory

The story of King Solomon, the successor of David, is both complex and confusing. One tradition maintains that he was the second son born to Bethsheba and David (2 Sam 12:24); another suggests that there were children born to them before Solomon (1 Chr 3:5). In one place the child is called Solomon (2 Sam 12:24); in the very next verse the name given is Jedidiah (12:25). The wisdom that Solomon received from God is said to have been legendary, "as vast as the sand on the seashore" (1 Kgs 5:9), yet the burden of taxation he placed on the backs of the northern tribes precipitated their secession from the Davidic kingdom (1 Kgs 12:4). These discrepancies can only be explained by remembering that the "history" of this king, like most of the narrative material in the Old Testament, is really a collection of traditions that originated at various times and in various places, all for theological rather than historical purposes, and hence do not always concur.

The account of David's life and exploits ends with his last words to Solomon, his successor. While the aged king exhorts his son to be faithful to the covenant made with God, he also directs him to avenge blood wrongfully shed and to eliminate anyone in the court who might be a potential foe. Solomon is quick to comply with these directives. Though

Solomon is known as a king who secured his throne by use of the sword, he is most noted for his wisdom, the building of the Temple, and his extraordinary number of wives and concubines. While some of the details surrounding these latter narratives may not be rooted in historical fact, it is the meaning behind the accounts that holds the most significance.

There is an important body of literature in the Bible known as the Wisdom tradition. It purports to be a compilation of the wise sayings of Solomon (Prov 1:1; 10:1; 25:1). Various explanations are seen for this claim of authorship. (Some of them will be addressed in Part Two.) There are two well-known stories that may have played a part in strengthening this claim. One is Solomon's prayer for an understanding heart, and the other is the account of his decision to cut a baby in half in order to resolve an argument over parentage.

Once royal rule is securely in Solomon's hands, he turns his attention to the organization of his administration. He has not yet undertaken the building of the Temple, and so he goes to Gibeon to offer sacrifice to God. It is there that he has an experience of God. In a dream God invites Solomon to ask for anything he might desire, and God promises to grant the king's request. Solomon's request reflects unabashed piety and wholehearted commitment to God. Rather than ask for wealth or victory over his enemies, Solomon asks for "an understanding heart to judge your people and to distinguish right from wrong" (1 Kgs 3:9). The story says that God was so pleased with the king's request that in addition to the understanding heart, God granted Solomon wealth and glory that would rival the riches of any other king (3:13).

There is a curious perceived relationship between prosperity and wisdom held by ancient Israel that will help us appreciate how Solomon's reputation as a sage might have developed. It is rooted in the theory of retribution, which claims that goodness will be rewarded and wickedness will be punished. A second corollary developed out of this first one. It suggests that prosperity is actually evidence of goodness, and misfortune is clearly the result of iniquity. It stands to reason that the wealthiest person in the realm would be the king. Therefore, from this point of view, one might conclude that the king is the wisest person in the realm as well.

There is another reason why Solomon would be associated with the Wisdom tradition. It was during his reign that the nation of Israel began to take on the monarchic characteristics of the day, one of which was the development and growth of a substantial literary tradition. We have already seen passages that refer to Solomon's relationship with this tradition. The literary flourishing that took place under his rule explains the tradition's caricature of Solomon's wisdom.

The story about the baby claimed by two women (1 Kgs 3:16-27) is probably simply a well-known folktale included here to demonstrate Solomon's insight and fair judgment. Knowing that the real mother would relinquish her claim, the king offers to cut the baby in half so that each would have something. Scholars have discovered almost twenty versions of this popular story in various cultures. The original general character of the tale is seen in the anonymity of the king, a striking difference in a collection of stories in which all others explicitly identify him as Solomon. This should in no way be seen as a form of deception. Traditional people such as ancient Israel are frequently more interested in characterizations that capture the essence of one's traits than in historical accuracy that reveals very little. A story like this casts into bold relief the kind of acuity needed in a leader.

The tradition that links Solomon with the building of the Temple is not only grounded in history, but it also enjoys religious legitimation. It is first found in the story of the prophet Nathan's report of God's message to David: ". . . your heir after you . . . it is he who shall build a house for my name" (2 Sam 7:12-13). Once Solomon's political administration begins to take shape, he turns his attention to the building of the Temple. What appears to be a detailed building program is most likely a description of the finished edifice. The structure is made of cedars and fir trees from Lebanon and quarried stone. The interior walls are overlaid with gold or covered with carved figures of cherubim, palm trees, and open flowers. It is a magnificent work of art and a witness to the devotion of the Israelite people. The Temple becomes the visible sign of the presence of Israel's invisible God in the midst of the people.

There is a shadow in this story of glory, though. The demonstration of Solomon's royal authority and the nation's move toward international acclaim are accomplished by means of forced labor (1 Kgs 5:27-32), which sows seeds that will later grow into discontent and, perhaps, contribute to the division of the kingdom.

Upon the completion of the Temple, Solomon decrees that the ark of the covenant be brought into the Temple, where it is installed in the sanctuary. In accord with the ancient tribal tradition, the presence of the ark establishes the Temple as the major shrine in Israel. Then the glory of the Lord fills the Temple, indicating that God has indeed taken up residence there. The prayer of Solomon that marks this occasion includes petitions for protection from both military defeat and natural disaster. The celebration lasts for eight days. At its completion God appears to Solomon once again and reinforces the conditional nature of the covenant agreement: "If you and your descendants ever withdraw from me . . . I will cut off Israel from the land I gave them and repudiate the Temple I have consecrated to my honor" (1 Kgs 9:6-7). Like so many passages we have examined, this one probably reflects a much later period, perhaps the time of the Exile, when the nation was experiencing the very misfortune described here.

The magnitude of Solomon's harem is legendary: "He had seven hundred wives of princely rank and three hundred concubines, and his wives turned his heart" (1 Kgs 11:3). A contemporary person might mistake the love referred to as romantic love. The Hebrew word can mean "commit," as in a legal contract. Someone from the ancient world would marvel at the wealth of the man and the extent of his foreign alliances. Solomon's wives are "of princely rank." Most likely this means that he has sealed several treaties with a marriage to one of the daughters of the treaty partner. Being "of princely rank," these wives would have brought their religious practices with them and, perhaps, even some of their idols. In other words, Solomon is not only in league with foreign nations, but he has opened the door to idolatry in the land of Israel.

The text tells us that "his wives had turned his heart to strange gods, and his heart was not entirely with the LORD, his God" (1 Kgs 11:4). From this point in the story forward, Solomon's devotion to God becomes more and more tainted. Finally God tells him that his kingdom will be torn apart. Adversaries rise up around him. One in particular, Jeroboam, spearheads the defection that will split the kingdom.

CHAPTER FIVE

A Kingdom Divided

To your tents, O Israel

As stated in the previous chapter, many of Solomon's extraordinary accomplishments had deleterious consequences. His reorganization of the kingdom into political districts may have resulted in more efficient management, but it also disregarded tribal boundaries and thereby undermined traditional tribal loyalties. Solomon's marriages to foreign women may have solidified several of his international treaties, but they also introduced foreign gods into Israel.

Solomon's building projects, particularly the Temple in Jerusalem and the pools and aqueducts that supplied necessary water to the city (the remains of which can still be seen today, though some claim that they were really built at the time of Herod), were certainly engineering feats. They required vast amounts of building materials and a monumental work force. Natural resources were confiscated, and forced labor, or corvée, was implemented.

All this resulted in deep-seated resentment and tremendous financial burden, which the monarchy attempted to alleviate by means of heavy taxation. A significant share of this burden was imposed on those who lived in the prosperous northern regions of the kingdom. It appears that these people were forced to pay for what the southern inhabitants were able to enjoy.

Such policies were not merely socially and politically offensive, but they also violated certain religious prescriptions. Many believed that the king had no right to disregard tribal boundaries, since it was God who had set them in the first place (Num 34:1-2). The introduction of foreign gods into the land was a more serious offense, for only the God of Israel was to be worshiped in the land of Israel. As for the circumstances surrounding the building of the Temple, forced labor was particularly abhorrent to a people whose very identity rested on the claim that they were free and independent, liberated by their God to live in this freedom forever. The idea that their own king, the one chosen by God to ensure this freedom, would force them into projects not unlike the construction of Egyptian cities that was forced on their ancestors (Exod 1:11) challenged the very core of their religious distinctiveness.

In many ways Solomon eroded the unity and the pride within the people of Israel established by David. With the death of Solomon, the nation was at a crossroad. Rehoboam, Solomon's son and heir, went up to Shechem, an ancient northern shrine, to secure the allegiance of the northern tribes. The people prevailed upon him to lessen the heavy burden of taxation that had been placed on them by his father (1 Kgs 12:4). That was the only condition they required of him. If he agreed to this request, he would be assured their fealty.

Rehoboam consulted the elders who had been in the service of his father. They advised him to acquiesce and thus gain the loyalty of these people. The king also consulted some younger advisers, men who lacked the experience of the former group. They directed him to show strength rather than leniency. According to them, such strength would ensure fear and subsequent obedience. Rehoboam followed the advice of the younger counselors, threatening even stronger measures than those enacted by his father.

In response to the king's intransigence, at this shrine made sacred by their ancestor Abraham (Gen 12:6), the people refused to grant their allegiance and broke away from the jurisdiction of the Davidic king with the words:

> What share have we in David?
> We have no heritage in the son of Jesse.
> To your tents, O Israel!
> Now look to your own house, David (1 Kgs 12:16).

This was not only a political break from the legitimate, though irresponsible, rule of the monarchy; it was also a religious upheaval, for the heir of the house of David was regarded as God's chosen one

(2 Sam 7:12-16). The cry "To your tents, O Israel!" was a call to reconstitute tribal affiliation and to reestablish the prominence of ancient tribal religion. Such religion acknowledged God as the true and only sovereign. It was not a call to a new religion, but a return to the fundamentals of prevailing Yahwistic commitment.

In that earlier religious worldview, no family claimed royal privilege. Leadership was not inherited; it was demonstrated and then acknowledged. Kings were chosen by God, as were Saul and David, not by birth, as were Solomon and Rehoboam. Traditional shrines were reopened, and local priesthoods were reconstituted so that the people could worship God in places other than Jerusalem. Since the northern tribes maintained that the monarchy had failed in its political and religious responsibilities, they interpreted this move as a kind of reform. The government and people in the south, on the other hand, viewed this as political insurrection against the monarchy and a religious revolt against God.

Just as there is a tradition granting divine legitimation to the Davidic monarchy (2 Sam 7:12-16), so there is a similar tradition conferring divine legitimation on the kingdom formed by the separated tribes of the north (1 Kgs 11:26-39). This legitimation is associated with a former loyal and industrious servant of Solomon named Jeroboam. One day he comes upon a prophet named Ahijah, who, acting in a prophetic manner, tears his cloak into twelve pieces, each piece representing one of the twelve tribes of Israel. The prophet directs Jeroboam to take ten pieces, telling him, in prophetic speech, that God is going to tear away the tribes from the grasp of Solomon. Only his own tribe, the tribe of Judah, would remain with that king. (It is not clear what happened to the twelfth tribe. Some commentators believe that there is an allusion here to the tribe of Levi, which was not allotted land [Deut 10:8-9]. However, there is evidence that the tribe of Benjamin was also under Davidic rule [2 Chr 11:12].) Jeroboam organizes a coup to overthrow the reign of Solomon. It fails and he has to flee to Egypt for safety. It is only after the northern tribes separate from the Davidic monarchy that he is asked to be their king (1 Kgs 12:20).

The names of the two kingdoms, Judah and Israel, can be traced back to early tribal names. Originally, Israel was the name of a group of tribes that occupied the central part of the country, most likely the tribes of Joseph (Ephraim and Manasseh) and Benjamin. At a later time in the process of tribal affiliation, when Israel came to be identified with Jacob, the entire people was known as "the children of Israel." At the time of separation, the Davidic monarchy came to be known as Judah, the name of the tribal ancestor of the Davidic house. The northern organization retained the name Israel.

One of the first decisions made by King Jeroboam was the establishment of two major shrines in the North (when North or South are capitalized, the reference is to kingdoms, not merely directions), one close to the northern boundary at Dan, the other at the southern border at Bethel. This was done to prevent the people of the North from going to the Temple in Jerusalem. Worship there might renew their religious bonds with the Davidic kingdom. At both northern shrines Jeroboam set up a representation of a golden calf, an ornate pedestal intended to act as a fitting stool upon which the invisible God of Israel sat enthroned. These calves were never meant to serve as representations of God or of gods themselves, contrary to the accusations made by the southern kingdom (Exod 32:1-29). They were merely pedestals.

An important point should be noted here. When reading stories about the northern kingdom, it is important to discern, as far as this is possible, the origin of the account. A northern perspective will interpret the described events in as positive a light as possible; the opposite will be true if the tradition originated in the South. Since the southern kingdom judged the separation as religious apostasy as well as political rebellion, its version of stories about the North will usually be very negative. As we will see later, the final editing of the Bible was done in southern circles.

Because of the sins of Jeroboam

Most of what we know of the northern kingdom of Israel comes to us from the Deuteronomistic interpretation of Israelite history (see pp. 43–44). Though the earliest prophetic focus of this tradition probably originated in the north, it took on a southern perspective when it was brought down to the South after the collapse of the northern kingdom in 722 B.C. The disapproving evaluation of most of the northern kings springs from this southern perspective. King after king is rebuked for having perpetuated the sins of Jeroboam (1 Kgs 15:30, 34; 16:2, 7, 19, 26, 31; 2 Kgs 3:3; 10:29; 13:6, 11; 14:24; 15:9, 18, 24, 28; 17:22). And what were these sins? As stated above, Jeroboam set up altars at some of the northern high places or shrines, specifically at Dan and Shechem, leading the people in the north to worship at these shrines rather than in the Temple in Jerusalem. The southern Deuteronomistic point of view suggests that this worship was syncretistic and, therefore, false worship.

The establishment of the dynasty in the south provided a degree of stability to that monarchy. One knew from which family the next ruler would come. What was not always known was precisely which son would be heir to the throne. (2 Samuel 9–2 Kings 2, known as the Succession Narrative, recounts the struggle over succession that took place in David's own family; see p. 63.)

With the exception of the houses of Omri and Jehu, such monarchic stability was unknown in the North. Most of those kings came to power by means of coups. The length of their reigns spanned from a period of forty-one years in the case of Jeroboam II (786–746 B.C.) to one week for Zimri (876 B.C.). These northern kings are frequently characterized as charismatic in contrast to the southern dynastic rulers. This means that they gained the throne through some ruse or ability, not always admirable, rather than through descent within a family. Many of them lost power to another as quickly as they had grasped it from their predecessor.

Since the northern kingdom lacked the stability that the southern dynasty ensured, succession to the throne was always a pressing concern. The theme of trust in God, so prominent in much of the theology of the North, played a major role in its understanding of leadership as well. The story of Abraham's obedient response to God's directive to kill Isaac is an example of this. This ancestral story has been interpreted in various ways. Some believe that it contains remnants of the move from child to substitutionary sacrifice. We know that in the ancient Near East firstborn sons were often sacrificed and their bodies buried in the foundation of a building to ensure the prosperity of that city. The remains of such burials have been found in the ruins of Jericho. The story of Abraham and Isaac certainly depicts such a move.

On the other hand, the biblical text itself states the theme of the narrative: "God put Abraham to the test" (Gen 22:1). However, we know that stories about the ancestors are really stories about the whole people. Therefore, willingness to sacrifice an heir and to trust that God will provide has communal implications as well. The North may not have had the assurance of an heir to lead it, but its theology would have the people believe that God would provide.

The theme of a son in danger is also found in the Joseph cycle (Gen 37–47). This set of stories contains several themes that enhance the status of the North. Joseph was certainly a son in danger. In fact, all his brothers (the tribes of Israel) conspired against him. He was not the son chosen to father the monarchy; Judah was. Nevertheless, Joseph rose to prominence in the broader world and, by saving his brothers, actually saved Israel. While he was renowned as a hero by all the people, the North claimed him in a certain way. There is a story that describes how Jacob, on his deathbed, gave a blessing to Ephraim and Manasseh, the sons of Joseph (Gen 48). At that time Jacob told Joseph: "I give to you, as to the one above his brother, Shechem, which I captured from the Amorites with my sword and bow" (Gen 48:22). This account provides legitimation to Shechem, the northern shrine and later capital of the North. Finally, the northern kingdom itself is often called Joseph (Ps 80:1; Ezek 47:13) or Ephraim (Ps 60:9; Jer 31:9).

One of the most significant northern kings was Omri (876–869 B.C.). He established a dynasty that lasted for thirty-four years, enduring through three successors—Ahab, Ahaziah, and Joram. It was Omri who moved the capital city from Tirzah, a city with a history of death and destruction (1 Kgs 14:17; 16:16), to Samaria, a place that was strategically situated, easily defended, unoccupied, and with no tribal loyalties. Many commentators believe that this move marked a new chapter in the history of the northern kingdom. They also maintain that Omri was to the kingdom of Israel what David was to Judah. He brought stability and prosperity to this troubled land. His fame was acknowledged by neighboring nations. His peaceful acquisition of land in Transjordan (east of the Jordan River) is recorded on a Moabite stele (memorial stone). Even after his death Assyrian documents referred to Israel as "the house of Omri." One alliance he established resulted in the marriage of his son Ahab to Jezebel, the daughter of the king of Sidon, a union that was harshly criticized by the Deuteronomistic editor (16:31).

Ahab followed his father and ruled Israel for nineteen years (869–850 B.C.). He established himself as an able military leader as well as a firm administrator. He joined eleven other states in halting the march of the Assyrian king Shalmaneser at Qarqar on the Orontes River. Royal inscriptions claim that he sent two thousand chariots and ten thousand foot soldiers to that battle. While these numbers may be an example of literary exaggeration, they provide an insight into the man's international significance.

Ahab is best known for his marriage to Jezebel and his capitulation to her intrigue in the matter of Naboth's vineyard (1 Kgs 21). In this account Ahab wishes to annex this vineyard to the palace property. Naboth refuses to sell on the grounds that it is ancestral land, and as such he is required to keep it as part of the heritage of his family. As an Israelite, the king should have known and upheld this policy. His dejection at having been denied his desire infuriates his wife. Since she does not feel bound to an Israelite policy, she sets out to procure the vineyard through devious means. Naboth is falsely accused of blasphemy and treason. He is put to death, and the crown confiscates his land. Ahab now has the land he desired.

The injustice of this act is not allowed to go unrequited. Elijah the prophet is sent by God to announce judgment on the king. He tells Ahab that someday in the future, dogs will lick up the blood of the king in the very place where dogs licked up the blood of the innocent Naboth. Dogs will also devour the body of Jezebel. Ahab repents and does penance for his part in this sinful act. God does not totally relent; he does not afflict the repentant Ahab himself but postpones the punishment until a time in the life of one of his descendants (1 Kgs 21:19, 23, 29). This descendant is Joram (Jehoram), who is assassinated by Jehu, his commander-in-chief. His bloody body is cast into the field of Naboth (2 Kgs 25–26), and his death ends the Omride dynasty.

Jehu ruled in Israel for twenty-eight years (843–816 B.C.). He established a dynasty that lasted through five generations and ninety years. He is remembered as a religious reformer. He waged a constant war against the worship of the Tyrian god Baal, which had been introduced into Israel by Jezebel and fostered by her son Ahaziah (1 Kgs 22:52-54). Jehu destroyed the temple dedicated to Baal and the idols found in it (2 Kgs 10:27). With the death of Zechariah, the last member of Jehu's dynasty (745 B.C.), the northern kingdom began a rapid decline, which ended in 722 B.C. with its defeat at the hand of the Assyrians.

The man of God

Two men loom large on the horizon at this time in the history of the northern kingdom. They are the prophets Elijah and Elisha. Although they left no record of prophetic oracles, as did many of the later prophets, these men are known for several remarkable exploits. Elijah exemplifies the strictest traditions of Yahwism. He railed against idolatry; he stood up against the exploitation of the vulnerable; and he was solicitous toward the poor. Elisha was the chosen successor of Elijah. Though at times his character appears to be somewhat questionable, he is remembered as a worker of miracles.

Five major stories epitomize the prophet Elijah, whose name means "my god *(eli)* is the LORD *(jah)*." Two important stories recount events surrounding a drought that was predicted by the prophet himself. He has been living an ascetic life in a wadi, a dried-out riverbed where there is still a small stream of water. There he is sustained by bread and meat brought to him by ravens. Directed by God, he moves to Zarephath in Sidon (1 Kgs 17:7-24). There he meets a poor widow, who, with the last remnants of flour and oil, is about to prepare some bread for herself and her son. Elijah asks for the little bread and water she has. Though in dire need herself, she complies and is rewarded with a constant supply of flour and oil. Sometime later the son of the woman falls mortally ill. Stretching himself out on the child, the prophet prays to God, and the boy is restored to life. These stories must have come to mind when Jesus spoke of the widow in the Temple who gave the little bit that she had (Luke 21:3) and when he raised to life the son of another widow (Luke 7:12-15).

Perhaps the most dramatic event is the contest on Mount Carmel between Elijah, the only Israelite prophet who survived Jezebel's murderous purge, and four hundred and fifty prophets of Baal (1 Kgs 18:21-40). The drought is now severe, and the famine resulting from it is life-threatening. In desperation the people turn to any religious belief or practice that might assuage their need. They turn from worship of the one true God to a syncretistic religion that includes the worship of Baal, the Canaanite god of rain and fertility as well. The contest on Mount Carmel pits the presumed power of Baal against the sure power of the God of Israel.

Two young bulls are slaughtered and placed on the wood of an altar. However, the wood is not set on fire. Mockingly, Elijah entreats the prophets of Baal to call upon their god to send fire from heaven to consume the sacrifice. They do as directed, calling on their god from morning till noon, but to no avail. As the time for the evening sacrifice approaches, Elijah has both the sacrificial animal and the entire altar soaked in water. He then calls upon the God of Israel, who immediately sends down fire to consume the sacrifice. There is no doubt in anyone's mind as to the identity of the all-powerful God. The prophets of Baal are then seized by the people and put to death.

Jezebel is infuriated when told that all the prophets were put to the sword, and she vows to mete out the same fate to Elijah. When he hears of this threat, he flees to Mount Horeb (the name given to the mountain on which Moses received the commandments, according to the Deuteronomistic tradition). It is there that the prophet has a mysterious experience of God (1 Kgs 19:9-13a). Hiding in a cave in the mountain, he is called by God and told to stand outside, for God is going to pass by. At first there is a great wind, and then an earthquake, and finally fire—

three examples of natural phenomena believed to accompany a theophany (a revelation of God; Exod 19:16; Job 38:1; 40:6). However, God is not experienced in any of these phenomena. It is in a "tiny whispering voice" that Elijah recognizes the presence of God. Most commentators interpret this to mean that God is found not only in spectacular occurrences but also in the simple, everyday events of life.

Elijah is told by God to leave the safety of the mountain and the wilderness and return to Israel, there to anoint Jehu king. It is at this time that Elijah encounters Elisha, the man who will succeed him as "man of God" and prophet to the people of Israel. Elisha follows Elijah as attendant until the latter is taken up to heaven in a fiery chariot. Before this happens, Elijah is once again embroiled in conflict with Ahab and Jezebel. It is he who condemns both Ahab and Jezebel for the treachery they devised in securing Naboth's vineyard and who foretells the horrible end that each would face (1 Kgs 21:17-29). To the end of his life, Elijah is the champion of justice.

The account of Elijah's departure from this earth is described in miraculous detail (2 Kgs 2:8-11). When Elijah and Elisha arrive at the Jordan River, Elijah rolls up his mantle and, using it as a rod, strikes the river. The waters part, and the two men cross over on dry land. It is there that Elisha receives a double portion of Elijah's spirit, making him the prophet's legitimate heir. (Inheritance was divided into one more portion than there were heirs, and the eldest or primary heir was given double portion.) With that, a flaming chariot and flaming horses come between the men, and Elijah is taken into heaven in a whirlwind, leaving behind his mantle, which is to be taken up by his successor, Elisha.

The absence of any record of Elijah's death has resulted in many traditions, both Jewish and Christian, regarding his presence among us and his return before the end of time. The Jewish tradition honors him at every circumcision, designating a seat for him at the table. The same is done at the Passover, when a cup of wine is poured for him at the conclusion of the Seder meal. The book of the prophet Malachi states that Elijah will return at the end of this age to usher in the messianic era (Mal 3:23-24). This prophetic statement is behind the disciples' question: "Why do the scribes say that Elijah must come first?" To which Jesus replies: "Elijah will indeed come and restore all things" (Matt 17:10-11; Mark 9:11-12). This was a common belief in Israel. Many in the crowds believed that Jesus was Elijah returned (Matt 16:14; Mark 8:28; Luke 9:19; John 1:21, 25). Jesus corrected this misperception about himself by ascribing the Elijah tradition to John the Baptist (Matt 11:14;

17:12; Mark 9:13). Even Herod wondered about John's identity (Mark 6:15; Luke 9:8).

Of all the prophets in Israel's history, it is Elijah who came to be known as the embodiment of Israelite prophecy. This is seen in the accounts of the transfiguration of Jesus, where Elijah appears on the mountain with Moses, who represents the Law (Matt 17:3; Mark 4:9). Together they stand for the entire Israelite tradition, the Law and the prophets, giving legitimization to the teaching and actions of Jesus. The frequency with which the people at the time of Jesus refer to Elijah indicates the significance this man enjoyed in the religious tradition of Israel.

The prophet Elisha, whose name means "god *(eli)* is salvation *(sha)*," is presented in an entirely different light than is his mentor and predecessor Elijah. He is called to be a prophet by a prophetic act (1 Kgs 19:19-21). When Elijah comes upon Elisha working in a field, he throws his own mantle over him, signifying that Elisha would take up the work that Elijah has begun. Elisha immediately leaves the oxen and follows Elijah, but then is asked to say goodbye to his parents, a serious responsibility in a tight-knit, kinship-based society like ancient Israel. Elijah's response is cryptic, but Elisha's reaction is not. He not only leaves his former occupation, but he slays the yoke of oxen, uses the plow as wood for boiling them and gives the meat away. In other words, he makes it impossible to return to his former occupation. His commitment to the prophetic way of life is complete. (Jesus uses this episode as an example of wholehearted response to the call to discipleship; see Luke 9:59-62.)

Initially Elisha accompanies Elijah, but once he receives the double portion of Elijah's spirit (2 Kgs 2:9) and picks up his mantle (v. 13), he begins his own fifty-year-long ministry. Accounts of his miraculous powers are sometimes bewildering. At times he uses his powers for good purposes, as when he treats bad water with salt, thus purifying it (2:19-22). One account that portrays the prophet as a vindictive man who uses his powers for personal gratification immediately follows the account of purifying the water. While in Bethel, he is taunted by small boys for being bald. He turns on them, curses them, sending she-wolves to tear forty-two children to pieces (2:23-25).

Two stories in the Elisha cycle resemble an Elijah tradition (2 Kgs 4:1-37; cf. 1 Kgs 17:7-24). Creditors threaten to take the children away from a widow if she does not pay her deceased husband's debts. She asks for Elisha's help. He sends her back home to find that the oil in her jugs flows in such abundance that she is able to sell it and pay the creditors.

Elisha then seeks accommodations for himself and his servant in the home of a wealthy woman. Grateful for her hospitality, he informs her that she will bear a son. When this son is old enough to work in the fields, he takes ill and dies. Like Elijah before him, Elisha lies on a dead boy and brings him back to life.

The report of the poisoned stew is curious (2 Kgs 4:38-41). The prophet is responsible for the stew that contains poison, but then he transforms it by adding meal. There is no ambiguity in the account of the multiplication of the loaves. Elisha feeds a hundred men with twenty barley loaves, and there is some left over. The healing of Naaman, the leprous commander of the king of Aram, demonstrates the humility of the afflicted man and the power of the God of Israel (5:1-19). This miracle is meant to be a gratuitous act of divine mercy. Elisha's servant Gehazi sees it as an opportunity for personal gain. As punishment for his greed, he is stricken with leprosy (5:20-27).

Elisha's most important service to Israel is political in nature. He is instrumental in Israel's victory over the Moabites (2 Kgs 3:11-19); he counsels kings (6:8–7:20; 8:7-29). The prophet is usually remembered for his astonishing feats, though. Even his death is not devoid of the miraculous. Because of a Moabite raid, another body is hurriedly placed in the grave with the body of Elisha. When the other body touches the bones of the prophet, the man is immediately restored to life (2 Kgs 13:14-21).

As unorthodox as Elisha may have been, several Gospel stories are either reminiscent of events in his life or make explicit mention of him. The basic multiplication stories are similar, although the details within them are quite different. In the Gospel accounts there are many more than one hundred men and fewer than twenty loaves, perhaps an effort to enhance the miraculous nature of Jesus' miracle (Matt 14:13-21; Mark 6:34-44; 8:1-9; Luke 9:10-17; John 6:1-13). In another miracle account, Jesus refers to the healing of Naaman in order to demonstrate the all-encompassing nature of God's care (Luke 4:27).

The prophetic movement

Prophecy was not unique to ancient Israel. There is literary evidence that this phenomenon was common in other religious cultures as well. We might know prophecy best from the classical prophets whose messages are found in biblical books that bear their names. However, the teachings of most of the very earliest prophets were not preserved by their disciples for later generations. These prophets are better known for their actions than for their words.

The primary role of ancient Israel's prophets was the mediation and interpretation of what they thought to be God's mind and will. Some prophets received this message through dreams, visions, or ecstatic experiences, which then had to be interpreted. Others read signs in nature, like clouds, the flight of birds, or the entrails of animals. The unique gifts of the prophets were not their personal possession; they were given by God to be used for the community. In other words, prophecy was a component of ancient Israel's public religion.

Prophecy in Israel is often traced back to Moses. Two passages are particularly significant in this tradition. The first is found in the Book of Numbers. There we read that while in the wilderness, Moses complains to God: "I cannot carry this people by myself, for they are too heavy for me" (Num 11:14). In response, God directs Moses to select seventy elders to receive a share of the spirit that has been guiding Moses. They are then expected to assume some of the responsibility for the direction of the people. With this spirit comes the ability to prophesy: "And as the spirit came to rest on them they prophesied" (11:25).

The second passage is found in the Book of Deuteronomy. Moses instructs the people as to their manner of life once they enter the land of promise. He warns them against the soothsayers and fortune-tellers so prominent among the Canaanites presently living in the land. According to Israelite faith, such people manipulate mysterious forces, claiming to understand and even control divine power. In order to assure the people that they would still have access to God's will, he promises them: "A prophet like me will the LORD, your God, raise up for you from among your own kinsmen, to him you shall listen" (Num 18:15). It is to this mysterious prophetic figure, who later takes on messianic significance, that the crowds refer to when they wonder about the identity of John the Baptist (John 1:21, 25).

The early prophetic traditions refer to bands of prophets who seem to have roamed across the countryside together. We first meet them in the story of Saul, Israel's first king. After Samuel anoints him king, he is told: "As you enter that city [Gibeah-elohim], you will meet a band of prophets . . . you will join them in their prophetic state and will be changed into another man" (1 Sam 10:5-6, 10-13). These prophetic individuals did not gather haphazardly; they seem to have been organized into guilds (1 Kgs 20:35; 2 Kgs 2:3-15; 4:1; 5:22; 6:1; 9:1).

Five women are also identified as prophetesses: Miriam, Deborah, Huldah, Noadiah, and an unnamed woman in the Book of Isaiah. This is unusual in a society that is patriarchal in structure and androcentric in perspective. In the account of the deliverance of the people out of Egypt through the sea, Miriam, the sister of Moses and Aaron, is called a prophetess. Although there are several stories about Miriam, none of them describes her actual prophetic activity. She is simply identified in this role.

It is different with Deborah. She is described as both a judge (Judg 4:4-5), "judging Israel," and as a prophetess, mediating the word of God to Barak: "This is what the LORD, the God of Israel, commands . . ." (Judg 4:6). A rather cryptic verse in the writings of the prophet Isaiah states: "I went to the prophetess and she conceived and bore a son" (Isa 8:3). The reference is obviously to the wife of Isaiah. It is not clear whether she was actually a prophetess or is called one because she is the wife of a prophet.

Less known than Miriam and Deborah, but no less important, is the prophetess Huldah. During the reform inaugurated by King Josiah (640–609 B.C.), a copy of the book of the Law is found in the Temple. The contents of this book so disturb the king that he sends the high priest and several court officials to have the message authenticated: "Go, consult the LORD for me" (2 Kgs 22:13). Of all the prophets in the land at this time, they seek out Huldah. She authenticates the book and pronounces an oracle of doom, prefacing her prophecy of the destruction of Jerusalem in standard prophetic fashion: "Thus says the LORD . . ." (2 Kgs 22:16). As late as the postexilic period we find mention of a prophetess. Nehemiah rails against the prophets who act as obstacles to his work of rebuilding the nation after its return from Babylonian exile. The prophetess Noadiah is mentioned among them (Neh 6:14).

Prophets and prophetesses were men and women of their times. Their words and their actions could only be adequately understood within their respective social and political contexts. Some of them were attached to the court, advising the monarchy. Others functioned at the shrines, calling the people to appropriate fidelity to covenant commitment. They were always firmly rooted in some aspect of the religious tradition. With few exceptions, their religious convictions flowed from their Mosaic covenant foundation.

This is even true of those individuals who came to be known as false prophets. What made one a false prophet was seldom an error in the tradition itself, but insistence on the wrong aspect of the tradition at the wrong time. An example of this is Hananiah. When Jeremiah announces that God is going to punish the nation for its infidelity to Mosaic covenant obligations, Hananiah denounces him, reminding the people that God has promised to protect the house of David (Jer 28:1-17). Jeremiah calls for repentance for sin; Hananiah encourages false hope. The true prophet had to know which message was timely and which was not.

Northern theology

The scholarly hypothesis that identifies four major theological traditions in the Pentateuch—the Yahwist (J), Elohist (E), Deuteronomist (D), and Priestly (P)—has been severely criticized in the recent past. The presence of theological diversity within the first five books of the Bible has not really been questioned; only the claim that actual literary documents existed from which the Pentateuch was shaped has been challenged.

All agree that several theological perspectives can be detected. Parallel narratives describing the same or similar incidents (the wife of an ancestor placed in jeopardy in a foreign court [Gen 12:10-21 and 20:1-18]) have been found. Various divine names (LORD [Gen 2:7], God [Gen 1:1]) are used, and different mountains of revelation (Sinai [Exod 19:11], Horeb [Deut 5:2]) are mentioned. The theological perspectives uncovered throw light on some of the concerns of the people at different times in history and in different geographic areas of the nation.

It is generally agreed that the northern kingdom developed theology that came to be known as Elohist and Deuteronomistic. Although the Elohist tradition contains narratives about Abraham, Jacob, Joseph, and Moses, these stories are told from a very different theological point of view, a point of view that reflects the experience or need of the people of the northern kingdom (eighth century B.C.).

Scholars dispute the origin of the Elohist (E) version of the tradition. Some believe that these stories developed within the northern tribes at about the same time as similar stories developed in the South. Those who hold this position maintain that written forms of both versions were eventually brought together and edited after the destruction of the northern kingdom (722 B.C.). Other scholars argue that after the split of the kingdom (922 B.C.), leaders in the north adopted already existing southern traditions and reworked them to emphasize northern concerns. These are the traditions that were carried down to the South and incorporated into the national epic.

One aspect of this rich and dynamic incorporation of northern traditions into the traditions prominent in the South continues to puzzle scholars. While there are two northern versions of the Decalogue—E's version in Exodus 20:17 and D's slightly different version in Deuteronomy 5:6-21—no southern version of the Law has survived. This is particularly curious, since it was probably people in the south who incorporated the two traditions after the Assyrians had destroyed the northern kingdom.

The heroes in the northern or Elohist version are depicted as prophets who receive revelations from God. They are noble men, committed to God, the kind of men who can be held up as models for others to follow. Such characterization of national heroes encouraged the people of the North to accept leaders who were not found acceptable by the South. The attribute of God advanced in this tradition was divine transcendence. Divine revelation was seldom direct. It usually occurred through an intermediary, such as an angel, or through a dream or vision. The response expected of human beings was "fear of God" (Gen 20:11; 42:19; Exod 18:21). This tradition insists that exclusive commitment to God, not loyalty to a Davidic king, is the essence of religion.

As mentioned above, important northern shrines were established at Dan in the north and Bethel in the south. However, Shechem, a place in the southern part of the land apportioned to the tribe of Manasseh, continued to be an important religious site. Its significance can be traced all the way back to the ancestors. Abram built an altar there when he first entered the land of promise (Gen 12:6). Jacob settled there upon his return from the home of his uncle Laban in Haran (Gen 33:18). It was at Shechem that the covenant with God was renewed under Joshua's leadership, after he had led them across the Jordan River (Josh 24:16-27). Some scholars argue that Shechem continued to be the site of covenant renewal ceremonies. The very fact that Rehoboam went to Shechem to obtain the allegiance of the northern tribes (1 Kgs 12:1) demonstrates that even the Davidic king recognized its importance.

The centerpiece of northern theology was the covenant made by God through Moses with the entire nation at Mount Horeb (Deut 5:2), not the royal covenant made with the son or descendant of David, as is found in the Yahwist tradition of the South (2 Sam 7:12-16). At the time of the separation of the tribes, the North's return to a more Mosaic and tribal theological character was not an easy venture. Theology reflecting southern interests had been developing for almost eighty years, and people in both the south and the north had appropriated it. Many earlier tribal traditions must have been kept alive in the north during the Davidic structuring of the nation, for what has survived as northern theology manifests a clear Mosaic quality. An aspect of covenant theology that significantly influenced the way many historical traditions were remembered (Deuteronomistic theology) was retribution:

righteous behavior would be rewarded with blessing; sinful behavior would be punished with misfortune (see pp. 42–43).

While the northern reading of the ancestral and Mosaic accounts resulted in the Elohist tradition, the laws and customs that bear a northern character comprise what has come to be known as the Deuteronomistic (D) tradition. The development of this tradition is even more difficult to trace than is that of the Elohist. It is best described as a covenant perspective through which history is read. However, this history developed in at least two, some would say three, stages. This theological perspective is found in Deuteronomy, a book which appears to precede the historical traditions themselves, but which was probably finalized centuries later.

Israel's laws and customs are found in the Book of Exodus, a document that reflects the northern Elohist theology, as well as in Book of Deuteronomy, also of northern origin. The narrative context of Exodus is the encounter with God at the mountain and the establishment of the covenant, a part of which is the Law itself. On the other hand, Deuteronomy, which means "second law," is a second articulation of that Law. Presumably, it was given to a second generation of Israelite believers as they stood at the border of Moab, about to enter the land of promise. The entire history of preexilic Israel appears to have been told from the point of view of the theology of this book. Today scholars maintain that the book itself probably attained its final form around the time of the Exile. In other words, the Deuteronomistic theological perspective was operative long before the traditions that flowed from it took documentary form.

Scholars suggest that some form of occupation traditions originated in the north long before the Davidic monarchy inaugurated its theological enterprise. With the fall of the northern kingdom in 722 B.C., these traditions were brought down to the South with other viable northern theology, there to be consolidated with southern traditions, perhaps during the reign of King Hezekiah (715–687 B.C.). The reform launched by Josiah (640–609 B.C.) may have resulted in minor editing and amplification of this history. The final form emerged from the experience of the Exile. At each stage—the fall of the northern kingdom, the Josianic reform, and the devastation of the Exile—covenant theology denounced the sinfulness of the people and reminded them of their covenant obligations. Though originally a northern source, such covenant theology challenged the entire nation and eventually became a foundation stone in Israelite theology.

CHAPTER SIX

"Thus Says the LORD"

The decline of the northern kingdom coincided with the rise of a new and powerful Assyrian nation under the leadership of Tiglath-pileser III. He subdued many of the kingdoms of Mesopotamia ("the land between the rivers") and conducted a series of military campaigns designed to take complete control over Syria and eventually across the entire Fertile Crescent, including parts of the Egyptian empire. He succeeded in destroying Damascus and capturing much of the Galilee and Transjordan. Israel became a vassal of Assyria, and the Israelite king a mere puppet.

At the death of Tiglath-pileser, the Israelite king Hoshea renounced Assyrian allegiance and pledged his allegiance to Egypt instead. This move brought down the wrath of Shalmaneser V, Tiglath-pileser's successor. He laid siege to Samaria, the capital of Israel (2 Kgs 17:1-6). At his death, which some believed was the result of court intrigue, Sargon II took control. During the first year of his reign, he devoted himself to quell the unrest within Assyria itself. Only then did he set out to punish those vassal nations that had rebelled against Assyrian rule. Chief among them were Babylon and the Syro-Palestinian coalition, which included some of the northern cities of the kingdom of Israel.

The campaign against Syro-Palestine crushed all Israelite resistance. The policy of relocating conquered people was followed, and many inhabitants of the kingdom of Israel were taken into captivity, never to be heard of again. Those who remained were assimilated with other conquered people who had been relocated in the land of Israel. The area became a province of Assyria under the name of Samaria, and was governed by an Assyrian ruler. Judah was spared invasion because, throughout this entire period of turmoil, that nation had refrained from taking steps against Assyria. The classical prophets of the north should be examined against this political backdrop.

Classical prophets

We have already examined the biblical accounts of some of the early prophets, such as Miriam (Exod 15:20), Deborah (Judg 4:4), Samuel (1 Sam 3:20), Nathan (2 Sam 7:2), Elijah (1 Kgs 18:22), Elisha (2 Kgs 6:12), and Huldah (2 Kgs 22:14). Called by God, these women and men are remembered for the guidance that they gave to kings and military commanders, their criticism of disloyalty to the covenant made with God, or their instrumentality in manifesting divine power.

Another group of prophets that functioned in the eighth, seventh, and sixth centuries B.C. are remembered not so much for their exploits as for their communication of "the word of the Lord." These individuals are sometimes referred to as the classical prophets. They are more familiar to most people because their prophetic pronouncements were preserved by their followers, collected, enhanced, and handed down through the ages, and read during liturgical celebrations of both Jewish and Christian communities as part of their religious heritage. Some of these classical prophets were probably charismatic in the same sense as were the earlier prophets. They are primarily remembered for the prophetic teaching contained in the books that bear their names.

Classical prophets were grounded in the theology of covenant (see pp. 54–55). Their words called for fidelity to covenant commitment, whether they were words of encouragement or words of accusation. Though the message of the prophets has been preserved in various ways, the oracle is the primary prophetic form found in the Bible. Most oracles were probably relatively brief utterances. However, individual oracles were often gathered into larger literary units, giving the reader the impression of a lengthy proclamation. Words of encouragement are sometimes called "oracles of salvation"; words of accusation frequently take the form of "woes."

The political circumstances within which the prophets functioned influenced whether the message would be one of salvation and hope or one of accusation and condemnation. This explains why most preexilic prophecies were primarily messages of doom, while postexilic prophecies were charactistically hopeful. The politico-religious circumstances of the day often can be reconstructed from the content of the oracles. The people's sinful behavior or the hardships that they were enduring are revealed in the accusation or encouragement itself. Contrary to some popular perception, the prophecies were not fundamentally predictive. They were focused on the circumstances of the present, not on the future. The future was considered only as the consequence of the people's present response to the "word of the LORD" spoken by the prophets.

The very form of the oracle ("Thus says the LORD") has led some to posit a cultic origin of such formal prophetic speech. This idea is reinforced by the various references to a prophet's service at a shrine. Other commentators argue that the oracle is better understood as a form of lawsuit, thus placing the prophets in a kind of juridical setting. This notion corresponds with the element of judgment found in so many of the prophetic utterances. Regardless of the origin of the prophetic form, the narrative sections of the prophetic books show that the prophets themselves came from various social circumstances, and they functioned in many different politico-religious settings.

The prophets believed that they were communicating the words of God, and so they often prefaced their announcements with the phrase "Thus says the LORD" (Isa 7:7; Jer 2:5; Ezek 5:8; Amos 1:11; Zech 1:3). This introductory phrase underscored the prophets' insistence that it was God who was calling the people to repentance or encouraging them to remain faithful despite the hardships within which they found themselves. Their claim to be spokespersons of God rested in a profound conviction of having been called specifically by God to be prophets (Isa 6:1-8; Jer 1:4-8; Hos 1:1; Amos 1:1).

The message of the prophets that has been handed down to us has gone through a very complicated process of development. The major thrust most likely originated with the prophet himself (we have no prophetic books written by women). This teaching was probably collected by disciples (Isa 8:16), arranged in ways that could be easily retrieved by memory when necessary, and enhanced with narrative explanation and other supplementary material. Regardless of the date of the original prophetic activity or the editing done by the prophets' disciples, the final form of the prophetic books is exilic. Traces of postexilic editing are obvious in many of the books. Such modification was meant to ensure the message's enduring value. Though the prophetic teaching grew out of a specific politico-religious situation, as it was handed down and developed it continued down through the ages to call people to be faithful to their covenant commitment.

This complex compositional development raises the question of prophetic inspiration. If the message that has come down to us went through several stages of development and editing, at which stage did inspiration enter the process? Earlier understandings of prophecy often characterized the prophet as a solitary critic of society, the unique person who received some kind of direct and unique communication from God. While in many ways this view is correct, it is also significantly flawed. The prophets were people of their time, grounded in the common tradition of the people. They may have possessed a radical insight into the moral fiber of that people, but they were still a vital part of the community, shaped by its values and functioning according to its ethos. At times, as seems to have been the case with Isaiah of Jerusalem, they were part of the establishment. On the other hand, Amos appears to have been a marginal figure. The events of history also played an important role in the prophets' place in society. During times of safety and prosperity, they were generally marginalized. However, when danger threatened or hardship loomed on the horizon, they were accorded a more central role. In a very real sense, prophetic inspiration is found within the community itself.

Prophetic actions

Prophetic utterances were not the only way various prophets communicated the "word of the Lord." Some of them also acted out their prophecy in ways that appear to us to have been symbolic. However, the ancient people understood them and believed that these actions actually initiated the message the prophets intended to deliver. In many ways these actions took their toll on the prophets, for the messages concealed in symbolic actions were usually prophecies of condemnation and doom rather than of hope and salvation. This means that the prophets would act out in their own lives the punishment that God intended for the entire sinful nation.

Examples of prophetic actions abound. The collapse of the covenant relationship between God and the people of the northern kingdom is exemplified in the disintegration of the marriage of Hosea and his wife Gomer (Hos 1–3). The refined Isaiah, as he marched through the city naked, prefigured the utter shame of being herded way into the exile that awaited the people of Judah (Isa 20:1-6). The possibility that the exile meant not only displacement but also the real possibility that the Davidic kingdom had no future is typified by God's injunction to Jeremiah that he should remain celibate and not produce any offspring (Jer

16:1-4). The eventual flight of those who defended the city of Jerusalem while it was under siege is foreshadowed when Ezekiel, with baggage strapped to his back, dug through a wall and escaped in the darkness (Ezek 12:1-7).

Prophetic symbolism can also be seen in the names of some of the children of the prophets. These names include more than an etiological meaning, that is, one that explains something about the person who bears the name, such as Abraham, which means "father of many." These names have the same kind of prophetic meaning as do the words of the prophets. For example, as his marriage was falling apart, Hosea called the "children of harlotry" Lo-ruhama ("not pitied") and Lo-ammi ("not my people")—(Hos 1:6, 9). Isaiah's son's name, Shear-yashub (Isa 7:3), which means "a remnant shall return," was itself a sign of hope for the people.

Hebrew poetry

The prophetic oracles came down to us in poetic form. Ancient Hebrew poetry differs from English poetry in several ways. We are accustomed to think of poetry as speech organized in measured lines. Hebrew poetry, on the other hand, is quite different. The primary characteristic is its two-line pattern, the second line asserting or completing the first ("You who oppress the weak, and abuse the needy" [Amos 4:1]). The question of its poetic meter has been the subject of debate for centuries. The length of the syllable can mark meter by its accent or by the pitch used in pronouncing it. It is generally agreed that meter is a form of rhythm based on the repetition of sounds. However, rhythm can only be heard; it cannot be seen. The difficulty in assigning accent to the written verse of an ancient language with no living native informants is obvious. Furthermore, those who count accents do not always agree on which words are important enough to be considered. They ultimately agree, though, that the most common pattern is a 3 + 3 line.

Perhaps the most striking characteristic is the use of thought parallelism. This way of balancing the two lines is basically done in three ways. 1) The second line repeats in some way the thought of the first:

> Praise the LORD, all you nations!
> Give glory, all you peoples! (Ps 117:1)

2) The second line gives the obverse side of the thought:

> Ill-gotten treasures profit nothing,
> but virtue saves from death. (Prov 10:2)

3) The second line adds to the thought of the first:

> In you, Lord, I take refuge;
>> let me never be put to shame. (Ps 71:1)

As with all poetry, biblical verse employs various other poetic devices. The simile is a comparison between two objects marked by the use of "as" or "like" ("They were as tall as the cedars" [Amos 2:9]). Hyperbole is the deliberate use of exaggeration for the sake of effect ("his tongue like a consuming fire" [Isa 30:27]), and personification is the assignment of human characteristics to inanimate objects ("Wisdom has built her house" [Wis 9:1]). Hebrew poetry is noted for its play on sounds. In order to accomplish this it uses alliteration and assonance, the repetition of consonant and vowel sounds, respectively; onomatopoeia, the imitation of the sound actually made by the referent; and paronomasia, a pun or a play on words. Unfortunately, these features are lost in translation.

Perhaps the most significant poetic feature is the use of metaphor. Most metaphors compare two significantly different objects in order to uncover a particular characteristic that is obvious in one of them but not in the other. Every metaphor consists of three elements: the vehicle, the referent, and the tenor. The vehicle is the member of the comparison to which the characteristic naturally belongs. The referent is the other member, about which the comparison is made. The tenor is the actual characteristic of comparison. For example: "I am like a lion to Ephraim" (Hos 5:14). Here a characteristic (the tenor of the metaphor) of a lion (the vehicle) is attributed to the speaker, who presumably is God (the referent). The context of the passage suggests that the tenor or characteristic applied to God is the ferocity of the lion.

The relationship between the two objects being compared works in two different but related ways. In the first and more obvious way, a feature of one object represents a feature in an otherwise unrelated object. On another level, the association of ideas is based on emotional response rather than physical similarity. Here the poet is more intent on reproducing the emotional reaction, depending upon how the tenor is understood. When God's lion-like characteristics are meant to describe protection of the people, the metaphor can generate a sense of confidence and well-being. In the passage from Hosea, however, it is the disloyalty of the people that has prompted the metaphor. Here it is meant to create fear and dread, for the lion-like ferocity is directed against them.

A land flowing with milk and honey

According to the biblical story, the promise of a land flowing with milk and honey was first made by God to Moses when, speaking through the burning bush, God called Moses to lead the people out of Egyptian bondage (Exod 3:8). The possibility of inhabiting such a land became the motivating force that sustained them during their long sojourn in the wilderness. The scouts sent to reconnoiter the land of Canaan reported back, much to the delight of the people who had wearied of wandering, that it was indeed a rich and fertile land (Num 13:27). This land is further described in Deuteronomy 8:7-9:

> For the LORD, your God, is bringing you into a good country, a land with streams of water, with springs and fountains welling up in the hills and valleys, a land of wheat and barley, of vines and fig trees and pomegranates, of olive trees and of honey, a land where you can eat bread without stint and where you will lack nothing, a land whose stones contain iron and in whose hills you can mine copper.

A careful examination of the east-to-west topography of the land in the Syro-Palestinian corridor reveals four distinct regions: the coastal plain along the Mediterranean Sea; western highlands; the Rift Valley, formed here by the Jordan River and the Dead Sea; and the eastern highlands or plateau. These regions do not continue unbroken from north to south; rather, they are on a slightly tilted axis from north-northeast to south-southwest. This creates markedly different subregions. Several rivers run through the land, but they do not provide the kind of irrigation potential that the Nile in Egypt or the Tigris and Euphrates in Mesopotamia do. Consequently, the people of the land were dependent on rainfall for their own needs, as well as the needs of their crops and herds. The northern coast and the seaward slopes of the highlands received the most rainfall and, consequently, were the most fertile regions. The windward slopes of the highlands and the Rift Valley received the least amount. As a result, less than half of the land was suitable for farming, and a high percentage of it was found in the north.

The fertility of this "promised land" was both a blessing and a curse. It certainly did provide the people with both sustenance and the resources needed to thrive. However, the very fertility became a source of temptation. Economic disparity resulted in the social abuses against which the prophet Amos railed, and Hosea condemned the people for taking part in the fertility cults that flourished across the land.

Woe to you . . .

Amos, who lived in the middle of the eighth century B.C., was the first of the classical prophets. He was a native of Tekoa, a small town in the hill country of Judah, just south of the Israel-Judah border. He was "a shepherd and a dresser of sycamores" (Amos 7:14). Having received his call to prophecy through a vision, he set out for Bethel, one of the main shrines of the northern kingdom. At that time the nation was thriving under the reign of Jeroboam II. This was a time of prosperity and expansion that might be compared to that of Solomon. Since the Assyrians had conquered Damascus, Jeroboam II was able to recapture all of Transjordan. He launched a series of building projects, which always meant taxation and generally included corvée, or forced labor.

At this time there was also a significant shift in land-tenure policies. The poverty of some inhabitants forced them to relinquish family land holdings, allowing the wealthy to amass huge estates. This practice was diametrically opposed to the tribal federation's insistence that land be allotted along tribal or family lines. The people believed that the land really belonged to God, and they only held it in trust. For this reason it was not to be bought and sold at will. The land itself provided the security and sustenance needed to survive. During this period of history the privileged became more and more influential, while the peasantry were disempowered and disenfranchised. It was to this socioeconomic disparity that Amos spoke.

We generally find the prophets interacting with the political establishment, with the king or members of the court. Amos, on the other hand, was embroiled in conflict with Amaziah, the priest in charge of the shrine at Bethel. Some commentators conclude from this and from the prophet's mention of other cultic sites such as Gilgal and Shechem (Amos 4:4; 5:5) that Amos was a cult prophet. He may have gone to the shrine to proclaim his message, but there is no indication that he had a significant role to play in the cult itself. Besides, he was a Judahite and the shrine was in Israel. Furthermore, the prophet himself disclaims any prophetic status: "I was no prophet, nor have I belonged to a company of prophets" (7:14). Amos saw himself as one who had been lifted by God out of his very ordinary life and commissioned to chastise those who had been swallowed up by the allurements and pleasures of prosperity.

The organization of the Book of Amos provides us with both the specific message of the prophet and clear examples of prophetic forms of utterance. The first chapters contain a series of judgment oracles against various nations (1:3–2:16). This is followed by unexpected words of woe against Israel itself (3:1–6:14). The last chapters contain vision reports (7:1–9:8a). The book concludes on a positive messianic note. Many believe that this messianic ending is an exilic addition that softens Amos's fundamental tone of doom.

Anthropologists tell us that some forms of speech are more than descriptions or exclamations. They actually possess a performative power. In other words, they accomplish what they describe (e.g., the words "I do" effect marital union). This is particularly true of blessings and curses. These utterances call upon divine power to effect what the words declare. Once the words have been uttered, their power begins to bring about what has been spoken. It may take a while for the desired end to be accomplished, but the people believed that it would eventually happen. This means that what appears to be the predictive character of prophetic speech (foretelling the future) is really the unfolding of the power set loose through the prophetic utterance.

The series of judgment oracles found in the first chapters of the Book of Amos suggests a very interesting scene. One can image the prophet standing up boldly at the shrine at Bethel and pointing to six nations that surround Israel, nations that were at some time a part of the Davidic-Solomonic empire, nations that have acted in ways that are offensive to God. When the prophet indicts Judah, rival of the kingdom of Israel and Amos's own nation of origin, the delight of the northern people must have been overwhelming. The prophet then points the finger of accusation at Israel itself. Because the bulk of the condemnation of Amos is directed toward Israel, the judgment oracles against the other nations, though deadly serious, may have been largely preparatory to the principal message.

The judgment oracles identify the offenses committed by the indicted nations as social sins, and the punishments meted out are also communal. The surrounding nations may not have been explicitly included in the covenant, but as vassals of the covenanted people, they would have been somehow bound to abide by the fundamentals of the Mosaic social code of behavior. Because they were indeed partnered with God in covenant, Judah and Israel would be strictly held to the prescriptions of the Law. Thus their disloyalty was doubly heinous.

All the oracles follow basically the same pattern: an announcement that the words of judgment originate with God ("Thus says the LORD"), an indictment of the crimes of the nation, and a statement of the punishment exacted. The indictment of crimes is stated in the form of a numerical saying (x and x + 1; "for three transgressions . . . and for four"), a form usually associated with the Wisdom tradition. The use of this form has led some to suggest that Amos was really a scribe. Again, his own admission of having a lowly background contradicts this. Rather, the form was probably quite common in the clan wisdom of the tribal villages such as Tekoa, the village of Amos's origin.

The initial judgment against Israel extends into a series of harsh words of condemnation. It is there that we find a graphic metaphor that implicates the affluent women of the nation as well as the prosperous men. These women are called "cows of Bashan," a reference to the exceptionally fine livestock raised in an area northeast of the Sea of Galilee. The cattle there have nothing to do but eat and grow fat. By referring to the Samarian women in this way, the prophet is implying that that is precisely what they do as well. The men are condemned for their ritual observance, which is perfunctory and devoid of devotion. The remainder of the prophet's condemnation is directed to the entire "house of Israel."

It is in Amos's denunciation of the northern kingdom that we find the first reference to "the day of the LORD." This was originally thought of as a day of punishment for the enemies of the people of God. The justice of God demanded that someday those who had oppressed God's people would experience God's wrath. With the denunciations of the neighboring nations by Amos, the people presume that this dreaded day is fast approaching. However, Amos then turns toward the Israelites and declares:

> Woe to those who yearn for the day of the LORD!
>> What will this day of the LORD mean for you?
>> Darkness and not light! (Amos 5:18)

A pattern can be detected in the visions that follow. God reveals a misfortune that will befall the Israelites and then explains its meaning to the prophet. It is in the midst of this section of the book that Amaziah, the official priest at the shrine at Bethel, denounces Amos as a seer and tells him to go back to Judah. It is in response to this reproof that Amos justifies his behavior. He insists that he is a simple man, called by God from his humble occupations to deliver the word of the LORD (7:12-15). With this reply Amos continues to recount the prophetic visions he received.

The condemnatory message of Amos ends on a note of hope: "I will not destroy the house of Jacob completely" (9:8). Throughout the prophetic writings, eschatological judgment is found linked with eschatological hope. The nation would be punished, but it would also be restored. The exilic character of this ending is seen in the verses promising the rebuilding of the house of David (9:11-12). Though Amos warned the northern kingdom of punishment for its disloyalty, the southern kingdom of Judah was not being threatened, much less destroyed.

Fertility in the land

Just as the prophet Amos denounced the economic disparity that had eroded the sense of communal responsibility in the northern kingdom of Israel, so the prophet Hosea deplored another violation of covenant life closely associated with prosperity. He was outraged by the people's involvement in the Canaanite fertility cults. We have already discussed the fecundity of much of the land in the north. It not only produced abundant crops for human consumption, but it was also able to provide sustenance for sizable herds of animals. A religious worldview prevalent in the ancient Near Eastern world generally contended that such fruitfulness was dependent on the pleasure of divine forces. In order to ensure fertility of the land, the herds, and within society itself, the gods of fertility had to be invoked or appeased in some way. Various fertility cults grew out of this conviction.

The fertility cults found in the religions of the ancient Near East were generally reenactments of myths that explained the changing of the seasons. These myths told the story of a mother-goddess and her male companion, who was sometimes her husband and at other times her son. In a common mythic plot found throughout the entire ancient Near East, the male deity died, like the vegetation, and was reborn again after some form of sexual union. This union was called *hieros gamos,* or "sacred marriage." The people believed that each new harvest was the fruit of the sexual coupling of the divine couple. They further believed that they themselves could profit from these divine life-giving powers if they participated in some way in that sexual union. They accomplished this by replicating the sexual act of the gods with cult prostitutes, both female and male.

Baal, which literally means "lord," is a general term like "god." It is also the name usually associated with the fertility god in the Canaanite pantheon, the deity whose cult was so attractive to the Israelite people. This god was believed to be the storm-god, whose rain germinated the land, enabling it to bring forth life. The cult of Baal annually celebrated this god's death and resurrection as a part of the Canaanite fertility rituals. These ceremonies often included temple prostitution. Baal's consort is also found in the biblical literature. The name of this goddess most frequently mentioned is Asherah (Judg 3:7); the name Astarte is also found (Judg 10:6).

During the drought that seized the land of Israel at the time, Elijah the prophet challenged the priests of Baal to see which deity was able to produce rain—Baal or the gods of Israel (1 Kgs 18:17-40; see p. 75). The outcome of this contest, which took place on Mount Carmel, demonstrated that the God of Israel, not Baal, controlled the rains and the forces of nature necessary for vegetation to thrive.

Participation in the fertility cults was a sin of idolatry, not one of sexual misconduct. These cults were established as a way of securing access to the powers of fertility, not for the sake of sexual license. The very first commandment in Israel's law states: "You shall not have other gods besides me" (Exod 20:3). Any violation of this commandment was considered a form of idolatry. Involvement with a cult prostitute publicly announced devotion to another deity. It further implied that the God of Israel did not exercise control over the forces of life. As zealously as some of the prophets tried to purge the land of allegiance to these fertility deities, we know that their cults continued even up to the time of the Exile (Jer 44:17-25).

Rejection of these fertility gods was particularly difficult because the Israelites shared the same agricultural needs as did the Canaanites who were still living in the land. Therefore, it seemed quite natural to turn to Canaanite methods to meet these needs. Israel's sacred calendar paralleled that of its neighbors. The barley harvest was equivalent to the Israelite Feast of Unleavened Bread, the wheat harvest happened at the same time as Pentecost, and the fruit harvest occurred in unison with the Feast of Booths. It may have been very difficult to distinguish between Israelite and Canaanite harvest celebrations. Besides, the God of Israel was chiefly characterized as a warrior God, not as a God who had power over nature.

A harlot wife

We know very little about Hosea the man other than that he, too, prophesied to the people of the northern kingdom sometime during the eighth century B.C., probably about thirty years after Amos did. We do know that he was a partner in a problematic marriage. We find mention of this in the very opening of the book that carries his name:

> Go, take a harlot wife and harlot's children,
>> For the land gives itself to harlotry,
>> Turning away from the LORD. (Hos 1:2)

Since the Bible usually employs a different word to designate a sacred or cult prostitute, "harlot" and "harlotry" imply illicit sexual relations sometimes, but not always, for pay. Recent feminist social-scientific analysis of the ancient world has uncovered insights that throw light on the meaning of these words. It argues that in strict patriarchal societies, not merely illicit genital behavior but any kind of behavior of women that threatens social order and patriarchal control could be considered harlotry. In such groups the procreative potential of women belongs to the group and not exclusively to the individual woman. The men in her family—first her father, then her brother, next her husband, then her son—are responsible for safeguarding that great resource, since the future of the entire group depends upon it. When the woman endangers this potential by any kind of unsuitable behavior, she is as guilty of sexual impropriety as if she had illicitly been engaged in sexual relations.

The details of a troubled marriage between Hosea and Gomer, his wife, are not as important to the meaning of the book as is the meaning of the troubled marriage itself. It is used as an allegory of the fractured covenant relationship between God and the people. The way that the prophet responds to his wife and to the three children is a kind of "acted-out prophecy." It demonstrates the manner in which God will interact with Israel. There is a movement from the intimate relationship symbolized by the marriage, through infidelity on the part of the human partner (Israel), to a divorce, and eventually to reconciliation and reunion. Theologically, the account moves from covenant union to idolatry, then from punishment to reconciliation and a new covenant.

The first three chapters of the Book of Hosea sketch the prophet's marriage and family situation. However, it is not always easy to tell whether he is speaking of his personal tragedy or of the breakdown of the covenant relationship between God and the people. For example, the phrase "the grain, the wine, and the oil" (2:10, 24) is a technical way of identifying the bounty of fertility sought by the people through the means of fertility cults. Is the description of desolation referring to the shame that Gomer will experience or the barrenness of the land that will afflict Israel? Actually, one need not make such a distinction. In fact, it is better that one not do so.

A major part of the richness of the poetry is its multivalent character. It can be read and understood on two levels. On one hand, "the grain, the wine, and the oil" and all the other riches may have been the wages paid for Gomer's harlotry. Hosea might be telling his wife that he is going to strip her of the riches she has received from her lovers. Then she will have to rely on her husband, as she should have done in the first place. On the other hand, they are the blessings of fertility bestowed by the deity who exercises power over them. So that Israel will recognize its true benefactor, God will strip it of these riches. Then the people will have to rely on God, as they should have done in the first place.

In a particularly moving passage, the prophet describes the steps that God takes to be reconciled with the faithless people:

> So I will allure her,
>> I will lead her into the desert
>> And speak to her heart. (Hos 2:16)

The reference is to the time and place in the past when God invited their ancestors into an intimate and enduring covenant relationship (Exod 19). Since that relationship has been fractured ("she is not my wife and I am not her husband" [Hos 2:4]), it is necessary to return to that place and reestablish that covenant relationship ("I will espouse you to me forever" [2:21]). This reinterpretation of Mosaic themes would have been very appealing to people in the northern kingdom. This had been their battle cry when they renounced allegiance to the Davidic monarchy and established themselves as a separate political entity: "To your tents, O Israel" (1 Kgs 12:16).

The barrenness and desolation of the desert epitomized the struggles the people had to face as they traversed the wilderness on their trek to the land of promise. There are two ways of understanding the meaning of desert as a metaphor. The conditions that the people had to endure often tested them to the point of despair and nearly broke their spirits. The very barrenness and desolation that constantly confronted them with their own insufficiency forced them in their need to turn to God for sustenance and support. It seems that the experience of having nothing but God helped them to see that they needed nothing but God. That place of hardship became for them a place of covenant-making. The place that was fraught with danger became a place where they experienced the loving protection of God. It is only appropriate that now God, after stripping the people of "the grain, and the wine, and the oil" of temptation, should lead them out into the desert, where nothing will distract them from the allurement of God.

Besides the husband-wife metaphor, Hosea also employs father-son imagery to characterize the relationship between God and the people:

> When Israel was a child I loved him,
> out of Egypt I called my son. (Hos 11:1)

Lest we misjudge the role played by fathers in ancient patriarchal societies, we would do well to look carefully at the description of God's solicitude, certainly derived from actual family custom:

> Yet it was I who taught Ephraim to walk
> who took them in my arms;
> I drew them with human cords,
> and bands of love;
> I fostered them like one
> who raises an infant to his cheeks.
> Yet, though I stooped to feed my child,
> they did not know that I was their healer. (Hos 11:3-4)

The tender passion with which God loved these sinful people is captured in the details of this metaphor:

> How could I give you up, O Ephraim,
> or deliver you up, O Israel? (Hos 11:8)

Once again the words of the prophet resound with a message of reconciliation. In fact, the book might be divided into three parts, each ending with the theme of reconciliation. The first part, chapters 1 through 3, develops the marriage allegory and ends with a return to the place of commitment, there to reestablish the covenant relationship. The bulk of the book, chapters 4 through 11, recounts the ways in which the people have transgressed their covenant responsibilities, and it concludes with the father-son metaphor. The last few chapters, 12 through 14, report yet more offenses. However, the people will repent and will once again enjoy the blessings that only God can give.

As we come to the end of the first volume of our survey of the Old Testament, we cannot help but marvel at the diversity of traditions that we find there. As different as these traditions might be, at the heart of all of them is Israel's fundamental belief that God was with them, to protect them and to provide for them. We see this conviction expressed over and over again, from the care with which the people were created, the mercy shown them when they sinned, and the blessings bestowed on them generation after generation.

The ancient Israelites characterized God in several different ways. Their God was first a deliverer, freeing them from bondage in Egypt. Eventually, they came to realize that the reason God was able to exert power in the land of Pharaoh was that their God was in fact the creator of the world. As such, this God held sovereign sway over all people in all places. They further believed that the creator who vanquished the cosmic powers of chaos at the beginning of time chose them as a special people and protected them from nations that threatened their security. Thus they perceived their God as deliverer, creator, and, when necessary, warrior.

The ancient Israelites traced God's choice of them all the way back to their earliest ancestor, Abraham. This choice was ratified by means of a covenant, first through Abraham and then through Moses. The legal contract made through Moses included a set of responsibilities, the Law, the particulars of which were expanded as the experience of the people required. This Law outlined a way of life that identified them as God's special people. It was the basis of the religious, social, and political dimensions of their lives. Their leaders, both religious and political, were responsible for seeing that they were faithful to this program of life. When these leaders failed in this, prophets arose from among the people to call everyone back to fidelity to covenant responsibilities. Regardless of the changes that took place in the lives of the Israelites, the one constant remained: God was there for them, to protect them and to provide for them.

The unfolding story of Israel explains why God was perceived in so many different ways. The God who was always there for them was experienced in the way the people needed God. God was a deliverer when they needed deliverance, a provider when they needed food and drink, a warrior when they needed military assistance, a judge when they needed discipline. God was there for them, however they might need God's presence and power. From all appearances, the ancient Israelites were a quite ordinary people who had an extraordinary perception of God. In the second volume of this survey, we will see how this dynamic development of divine characterizations continues.